This book may be returned to any Wiltshire
library. To renew this book phone your library
or visit the website: www.wiltshire.gov.uk

Wiltshire
COUNTY COUNCIL

LM6.108.5

Red polished ware plank-shaped clay figure, Cyprus, Early Bronze Age. In the collection of the Pierides Museum – Laiki Group, Larnaca, Cyprus.

Slab-built Ceramics

Coll Minogue

THE CROWOOD PRESS

First published in 2008 by
The Crowood Press Ltd
Ramsbury, Marlborough
Wiltshire SN8 2HR

www.crowood.com

Wiltshire Libraries & Heritage	
Askews	
738.14	£14.99

British Library Cataloguing-in-Publication Data
A catalogue record for this book is available from the British Library.

ISBN 978 1 84797 004 6

ACKNOWLEDGEMENTS

I am indebted to all those who have provided both illustrations and information for this book, and others who have helped in many different ways. Without their generosity of spirit it would not exist.

Typeset by Simon Loxley

Printed and bound in India by Replika Press Pvt.

CONTENTS

INTRODUCTION

Slab-building, together with pinching and coiling, is one of the basic methods of constructing ceramic forms. The distinctions between these three techniques are not however as clearly defined as might be expected. A combination of pinching and slab-building can be used where small irregularly shaped slabs are hand pinched or patted and then joined together to create a form. In coiling, individual coils can be flattened into strips, long, narrow, flat slabs of clay, before being joined successively to build a vessel or other form.

All the work discussed and illustrated in this book has in common the fact that it started out as either a single slab, or series of slabs of clay. There are conceptual sculptures on a scale suitable for interior settings; large-scale outdoor sculptures, including pieces which are also kilns; relief wall pieces; murals commissioned for the interiors of public buildings, and outdoor murals on a massive scale. There are also vessel forms and pots for use in the preparation and serving of food. This international range of work – including contemporary, historic and prehistoric pieces – is indicative of the versatility of slab-building and demonstrates the scope for personal expression that is possible using variations of this fundamental technique.

The book is divided into two main sections under the chapter headings of Sculpture and Vessels. (The section on sculpture includes

Clay tablet, Jamdat Nasr, Iraq, c. 3200 – 3000 BC. Height 11 cm. This tablet is written in an early form of Cuneiform script.
© ASHMOLEAN MUSEUM, UNIVERSITY OF OXFORD (1926.564)

some architectural ceramics.) Within these sections the working practices of contemporary ceramic artists are described, in addition to individual artists' inspiration for their work. Although all these artists use slabs as the starting point for their work, they employ many different slab-forming techniques, including: hand-pounding; rolling out with a rolling pin or a slab roller; cutting from regularly shaped blocks of clay, using a cutting wire stretched between two notched lengths of wood; repeatedly dropping a block of clay onto a floor or work bench; slapping a block of clay onto a flat surface whilst holding it by alternate edges, thus stretching the clay to form a slab; throwing flat discs of clay on a wheel; paddling slabs with a wooden paddle; pouring slabs and extruding slabs. The qualities that individual artists aim to achieve in their work have a direct bearing on the particular type of slabs that they choose to work with. Some like to work with very soft slabs in an effort to retain the qualities of fresh clay in their finished, fired work. Others prefer to use slabs in a firmer state, so that they are self-supporting as work progresses on a form.

In a historical context, flat slabs of clay were used in the earliest-known system of writing, in which both impressed and incised marks were made in soft clay with implements made from reeds. The raw materials required were readily available in the river valleys of Southwest Asia, and as C.B.F. Walker explains in his book on Cuneiform script, as the system is known: 'Clay can be easily worked into a suitably flat shape for writing on while moist, and if left to dry in the sun after being inscribed will

7

soon be hard enough to stand up to considerable wear and tear.' Initially, pictures depicting specific objects were made in the clay (pictographs). This method was gradually superseded by standardized symbols based on stylized representations of objects, with just a few marks to indicate each object. Cuneiform was in use in Southwest Asia before 3000 BC, and continued until approximately AD 75. During that time it was used for recording information in up to fifteen different languages. The clay slabs or tablets, which were generally rectangular or square-shaped, were inscribed on both sides and measured up to 30cm (12in) square. Many of the cuneiform tablets in museum collections worldwide owe their survival to 'accidental' firing, when the libraries or archives in which they were stored were destroyed by fire.

Recent research has revealed that some pots dating from a much earlier period than cuneiform tablets, which may initially appear to have been either coiled or thrown, were in fact formed from slabs of clay. The research carried out by Dr Pamela Vandiver in the USA, has established that Southwest Asian pottery dating from 7000 to 3000 BC was made by 'sequential slab construction'. Palm-sized slabs of local clay, to which materials such as straw, chaff and grass were added for strength, were patted out and then overlapped and joined to make, first the base of the pot, and then the walls. The base and lower wall sections were thicker as two or more layers of slabs were used in these areas, and the slabs were also larger in size. The walls became thinner and the slabs smaller towards the rim of the pot. Both the inner and outer surfaces of these pots were sometimes smoothed over with a slip made from the same clay body, which is one reason why it is not immediately apparent that they were in fact constructed from slabs. Changes in the way clay was prepared resulted in more plastic bodies and led gradually to the introduction of coiling, throwing and moulding techniques. However, this type of slab construction continued as the main clay-forming method throughout a vast geographic area that extended from Egypt to Pakistan, and Turkey to Mesopotamia, for thousands of years, with examples of this practice still in use today.

Additional examples of slab-building in historical contexts are discussed briefly in the introductions to the two main sections on sculpture and vessels. The choice of historic work to include was determined by both personal preference and the availability of conclusive evidence as to which ceramics were slab-built in different countries and periods throughout the history of pottery.

Traditional slab-forming methods are still widely used in producing functional pottery in many parts of East Asia. Slab-made tableware, being particularly appropriate for the presentation of the food of this area, is used extensively both in restaurants and private homes in Japan and Korea. In China, the technique of slab-building also continues as a means of producing pottery, and is used, for example, in the production of large porcelain forms at Jingdezhen in Jiangxi Province.

During the early days of the Studio Pottery movement in the second half of the twentieth century, throwing was by far the most popular making technique in use. While some studio potters included a few slab-built forms in their repertoires, often large, flat slab dishes that were formed on either hump or press moulds, slab-building was definitely regarded as a secondary method of making, and was favoured more by artists making individual vessel or sculptural forms.

However, during the 1980s and 1990s, and continuing now into the twenty-first century, the number of ceramists using variations of the slab-building technique exclusively in the creation of their work, has increased dramatically. One somewhat surprising development has been the production of entire ranges of domestic ware from slabs.

My aim in writing this book has been to include as broad and representative a range as possible of the work that is currently being produced within the scope of slab-built ceramics, and, in doing so, I hope to broaden perceptions of what can be achieved using this fundamental but infinitely expressive ceramic technique.

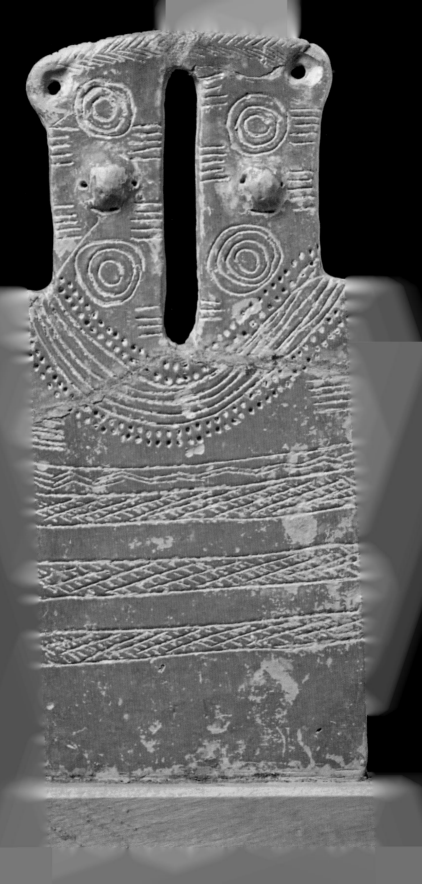

SCULPTURE

The technique of slab-building is particularly suited to creating sculptural forms, as asymmetrical shapes can easily be constructed, and has been used for this purpose at various periods and in different countries throughout the history of ceramics. Many of the fine examples of historic ceramic sculptures to be seen in museums were found in burial tombs, as it was a belief common to many ancient civilizations that the dead should be prepared for an afterlife by including various worldly goods or models of them, in burials.

In Cyprus, small elaborately decorated figures have been found in rock-cut tombs dating from the Early and Middle Bronze Ages (2300–1600BC). These 'Plank Figures' – flat slabs of clay that are generally no larger than about 27cm (10in) in height, are highly stylized depictions of the human body. Many are comprised of two rectangular shapes, one representing the head and neck, the second, the trunk (see frontispiece). Typically these figures bear incised markings that were filled with gypsum, representing hair, facial features, necklaces and belts. The nose is generally shown in relief. Some examples have two necks and heads on a single body.

During the Han Dynasty in China (206BC–AD220), much of the pottery produced consisted of earthenware funerary wares. By the latter part of the Dynasty, tombs of ordinary people contained models of everyday objects of

Red polished ware plank-shaped clay figure, Lapithos, Cyprus, Early Bronze Age. Height 24cm.

relevance to daily life, such as farm animals, granaries, pots and cooking stoves (see photograph on page 13). Included in many tombs were slab-built architecturally accurate models of buildings, ranging from humble houses to elaborate multi-storied watch towers and store houses.

These models, like all Han funerary wares, were made from loess (as were long stretches of the Great Wall of China and the Terracotta Army of Qin Shihuang). The low clay content and low firing temperature of loess meant low shrinkage during both drying and firing, characteristics that made it a particularly suitable material for use in slab-building. The copper green lead glazes on many of these tomb models (which were fired in oxidation) have over time become iridescent through exposure to dampness, and are now silvery grey in colour instead of a rich green. These replicas are of great interest as accurate representations of contemporary Chinese architecture. The Burrell Collection Museum in Glasgow, Scotland, has an impressive model of a storehouse, which was built in three separate sections and is almost a metre in height.

Slabs of clay have been widely used for architectural purposes in different periods and countries. In China, again during the Han Dynasty, extensive use was made of architectural ceramics in the construction and decoration of tombs. Large, hollow, slab-built bricks made from loess were used to line the walls, and also form the lintels and pillars of door surrounds. These bricks were decorated on the front face with stamped designs, forming bands of geometric repeat patterns as borders around

central pictorial motifs. It is thought that they were constructed around a supporting core made of wood, and that the stamped design was impressed before the support was removed. In typical slab-building fashion, the seams were reinforced with coils of soft clay. An example of this type of hollow brick in the Ashmolean Museum in Oxford, England, measures 122 x 33.6 x 12cm (48 x 13 x 4.7in). The bricks were fired to a temperature of approximately 1000°C in reduction, resulting in a grey coloured surface.

The use of pottery tiles was widespread throughout the Roman Empire (31BC–AD476). In addition to flat tiles used for roofs, walls and floors, specialist tiles such as slab-built, relief-patterned, box-flue tiles were also produced.

Model of a house, with a dog inside, early first century. Chinese, Han Dynasty (206BC–AD220). Earthenware, 23.8 x 29 x 20.8cm.

GIFT OF LILY SCHLOSS IN HONOUR OF GOLDIE STERNBERG, 2002. ART GALLERY OF NEW SOUTH WALES, AUSTRALIA (132.2002)

These rectangular box-shaped tiles were used for ducting warm air in the underfloor heating systems of both private villas and public baths. The purpose of the elaborate impressed patterns, often geometric in style, that are to be found on some tiles (including the example from the British Museum shown on page 14) and are thought to have been made using a wooden roulette, was simply to provide

Model of a storehouse, Chinese, Eastern Han Dynasty (AD25–220). Earthenware, three separate sections, height 95.2cm. The scale and complexity of this piece reflect the status of the occupant of the tomb from which it was excavated (near Shensi).

© GLASGOW MUSEUMS: THE BURRELL COLLECTION (38.98)

a textured surface as a key for the mortar or plaster in which they were set.

The contemporary artists whose work is included in this section use many different types of clay and firing processes to produce a very wide range of slab-built sculpture, including both free-standing and wall pieces.

Impressed brick, unglazed, Chinese, Han Dynasty 206BC–AD220. 122 x 33.6 x 12cm.

© ASHMOLEAN MUSEUM, UNIVERSITY OF OXFORD (1961.143)

13

***Romano-British box-flue tile. Earthenware
with relief pattern. Ashtead, England, UK.***

REGINA HEINZ

Regina Heinz, originally from Austria and now working in the United Kingdom, creates sculptures that engage on many different levels simultaneously. One is immediately aware of the strong forms and the small areas of primary colours in geometric shapes punctuating the surfaces, often in grid-like patterns. While much of her earlier work consisted of pillow-like rectangular or square forms that appeared to be inflated, some of the more recent sculptures are of more complex construction and also differ in character.

In captions accompanying images of Regina's work, the term 'soft slab construction' is frequently used. This accurately describes both the technique used to create the pieces and also their expression. The finished work retains the fresh appearance of slabs in their soft state as work progresses on a form. Regina explains that she has developed a slab-building technique that emphasizes the softness and tactile properties of the material:

> Slabs are rolled out, incised with a motif, moulded, shaped and then 'tailored' and joined until the piece has taken on its final shape and expression, yet the material has retained its original softness and surface texture. This technique is paramount to my work and requires both spontaneity and control, as the soft slabs react to every touch and record every imprint of the hand.

She continues:

> I am fascinated by the pliability and softness as well as the tactile and sensual surface qualities of clay and its ability to enclose a void, an empty space, which can be felt from outside. My aim is to keep exploring the nature of the material and to establish and refine my personal style through the combination of

In Perspective, *wall piece by Regina Heinz (Austria/UK), stoneware, 45 x 30 x 8cm.*

PHOTOGRAPH BY ALFRED PETRI. © THE ARTIST

form, the surface texture of clay and the effects of colour.

When preparing for constructing a sculpture, Regina uses a slab roller for making larger slabs, but the final rolling out is done by hand, with a rolling pin, on newspaper. The thickness of the slabs can be more easily controlled this way, and also the resulting imprints of creases from the paper enrich the clay surface with cracks and stretch marks. Grogged stoneware clay (Crank or White St Thomas) is used, as the grog content provides tactile and visual texture as well as strength during the forming process. A basic motif is incised into the slabs at this stage to provide the framework for the layers of coloured stains, oxides and glazes that will be applied later. Once the slabs are firm enough to work with, but still soft enough so as to be easily manipulated, they are placed over formers comprised of crumpled-up sheets of newspaper and chicken wire. Using these materials – particularly the newspaper – allows the slabs to be further articulated until a satisfactory form has been achieved. Additional incising of the motif may take place at this stage, and sometimes holes are pierced right through the clay, forming part of the motif. Cuts are then made from the edges of the slabs towards the centre,

in a process that Regina refers to as 'tailoring', in that it is similar to the technique used in making clothing to give shape to a garment. Once the main slab components are leather-hard, they are removed from their formers and placed on top of each other, again using crumpled paper as a support. The slabs are then assembled to form the sculpture, using narrow slabs of clay to join them. The paper support is removed before the last side slab is put in place. The basic stage of forming the sculpture has now been completed.

Originally trained as a painter, Regina eventually came to realize that working on a flat surface was not enough for her. Seeing an exhibition of ceramic sculpture, she explains that 'clay presented itself as the medium that would enable me to go beyond the two-dimensional representation, to give back to the images the third dimension that they originated from.' However, painting still plays an integral and essential part in her creative process through her use of both colour and drawing, and she cites the influence of abstract painters including Paul Klee and Piet Mondrian in her work.

The motifs incised on the surfaces of Regina's sculptures are primarily based on landscapes, including those of her mountainous home country of Austria, not in a literal

Regina Heinz attaching a section of the sidewall to a sculpture.

The completed form before biscuit firing.

PHOTOGRAPHS BY REGINA HEINZ

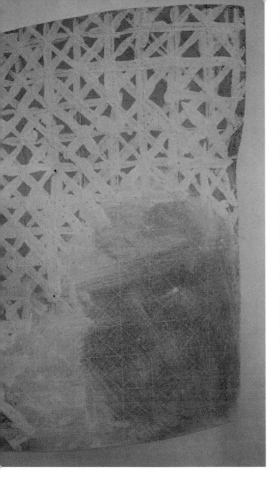

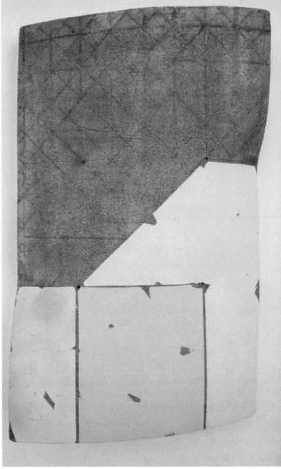

sense however. Having initially taken many photographs of particular surface details found in natural or manmade environments, the resulting photographic imagery provides inspiration for the geometric grid patterns, or compositions, that are the basis for the different areas of colours applied to the surfaces of the forms. To achieve the required surface effects, Regina explains that ' vibrant primary colours are applied over a base of neutral greys and whites, to enhance and reveal the underlying form, and to add to the sensual qualities of each piece.'

The forms are biscuit fired to 1035°C, after which a dark glaze (a Lithium-based glaze with added copper) is brushed into the incisions and holes and wiped off again so that it only remains in the grooves. A wash of iron oxide is then applied, and the piece is again fired to

A dark Lithium glaze is brushed onto a wall piece and wiped off again to emphasize the incised design.

A Lithium glaze is applied to masked-out areas. See also finished sculpture on page 15.

PHOTOGRAPHS BY REGINA HEINZ

1035°C. After this second firing, blue, grey or white Lithium glaze is brushed onto masked-out areas, applied in two to three thin layers (of a milky consistency). Some biscuit slips (blue, yellow) are also applied at this stage to emphasize certain parts of the pattern (usually lines, grids etc.). Masking tape is used to mask-out these specific areas where glaze or colours are to be applied, in order to achieve precise borders and patterns.

17

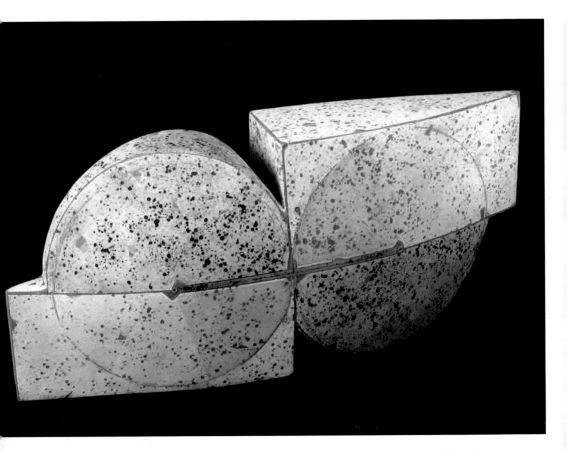

Engaged, *ceramic sculpture by Regina Heinz,*
2005. Stoneware, 30 x 65 x 12cm.

PHOTOGRAPH BY ALFRED PETRI. © THE ARTIST

The piece is then fired for a third time. If the pattern is complete at this stage, this will be the final firing. Often, however, a wash of blue ceramic pigment and more biscuit slips are applied over the fired base layer of glaze, before the form is fired one last time. So most pieces undergo a total of four firings, three glaze firings in addition to a biscuit firing, all of which are to a temperature of 1035°C. Regina explains that at this temperature the Lithium glaze is under-fired, the Lithium grains are just starting to melt and create an interesting speckle effect that adds depth and variation to the coloured surface.

Regina says of her work:

I think of my work as three-dimensional images, and my sculptures and wall pieces result from an ongoing process of research into the interaction of the flat and the three-dimensional. In my most recent work, I cut into the square clay slabs and by bending and altering the rectangular pillow- or box-like shapes, I discover new exciting possibilities of interlinking image and form in a more stringent way. My latest pieces combine the soft qualities of clay with a more complex architectural form and a precise geometric design painted on in vibrant ceramic colours.

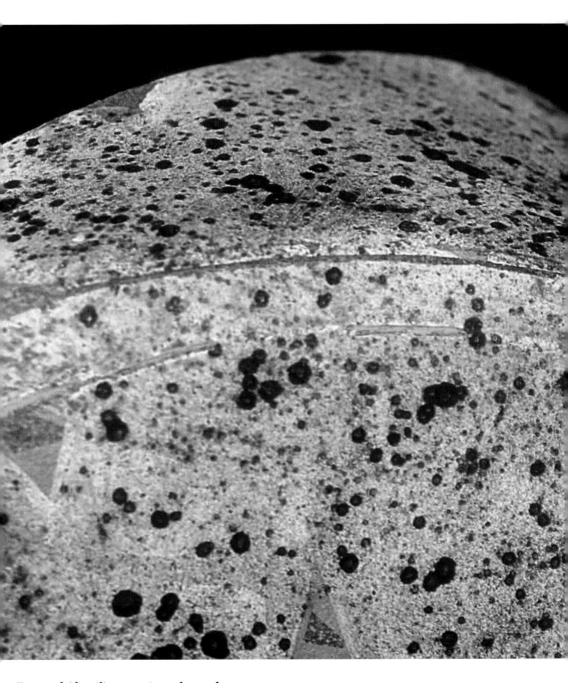

Engaged *(detail), ceramic sculpture by*
Regina Heinz, 2005.

PHOTOGRAPH BY ALFRED PETRI. © THE ARTIST

BARBARA CAMPBELL-ALLEN

Barbara Campbell-Allen's ceramic sculptures could be said to be a celebration of her homeland, Australia – specifically the wilderness landscape of Eastern Australia. The texture, colour and sound of the 'bush' captured in clay. In her words: 'The bush has been my playground all my life. As an adult I have walked, skied and "canyoned" from the Blue Mountains through to south-west Tasmania. These environments are my down time – my space.'

Barbara's recent work has included an installation for a touring exhibition that consisted of a series of slab-constructed forms, as she explains:

This work was commissioned for the exhibition 'Terra Alterius – Land of Another', where the brief was to create work in response to the

Old Rivers by Barbara Campbell-Allen (Australia), one of ten separate pieces in an installation. Porcelain, stoneware and earthenware clays, long wood-fired, 15 x 50 x 50cm.

PHOTOGRAPH BY PAUL CAMPBELL-ALLEN. © THE ARTIST

idea that Australia was not colonized by Britain as 'terra nullius', land of no-one, but recognized as being 'terra alterius', land of another. My slab constructions form an installation, *Old Rivers*, in which ceramic parts are intimate representations of places that together build my understanding of the Australian continent. Each component is a special place – self-sufficient, individual and unique. All pieces were wood-fired in a tunnel or anagama kiln. This firing process, whilst giving individuality to each piece, has a unifying effect by the blending of colour and texture.

In making the series of sculptural forms that together constitute the *Old Rivers* installation, Barbara used plaster press moulds in constructing the base sections of the individual pieces. These basic concave shapes, formed by joining slabs together, were reinforced internally, also using slabs. Paper clay was used in forming the bases to reduce cracking and to give strength at the bone-dry stage. It also allowed for an increase in scale due to its relative lightness. Measuring approximately 50 x 50 x 15cm (20 x 20 x 6in), each individual piece weighed up to 15kg (33lb) when completed. The slabs used to form the top sections were stretched by slapping them down on a concrete floor that had been sprinkled with Hallam fire clay. Sections torn from these stretched and textured slabs were then manipulated onto the bases to construct landscape-like folds, being beaten and altered in the process.

Barbara describes her inspiration for this work: 'The catalyst for *Old Rivers* is, very simply, my experience of the environment of Eastern Australia. I experience these places as pristine environments because of the "light touch" of indigenous Australians on the land. It is the

ABOVE: *Barbara Campbell-Allen stretching a slab by banging it on a concrete surface that has been sprinkled with fireclay.*

RIGHT: *Sections torn from stretched and textured slabs are manipulated onto the base, which is supported in a plaster mould.*

PHOTOGRAPHS BY PAUL CAMPBELL-ALLEN

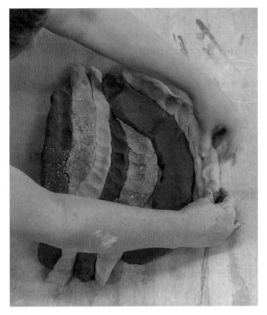 

Joining coils of different types of clay to form a slab, and rolling the slab.

PHOTOGRAPHS BY PAUL CAMPBELL-ALLEN

feather-light touch of indigenous people that has enabled non-indigenous Australians to experience this wilderness first hand.' She continues: 'The installation is an amalgamation of microcosms; a collection of memories and experiences. It is a plea for these memories and experiences to be available to future generations as it was to me, because of the relationship non-indigenous Australians have with their land, recognized or not.'

The pieces for the 'Terra Alterius' exhibition were fired in various sections of Barbara's 3m (10ft) long anagama (single chamber woodfire kiln), which she built in 1988. Learning how best to take advantage of the various surface effects that it is possible to achieve in her kiln has been an ongoing process for Barbara. At this stage, she knows what type of effects are likely to be achieved in specific areas of the kiln, and, consequently, makes pieces that are

appropriate in terms of form and the types of clays used, to be placed in the different areas.

The relationship between process and aesthetic is fundamental to understanding anagama-fired work. Dr Owen Rye has used the phrase 'Anagama – the Art of Uncertainty' as the title to an article that explored this relationship. This succinctly explains the working framework of anagama practitioners. I work within known parameters, accepting the vagaries integral to anagama firing, but capitalizing on the effects of the process. I fire the kiln for between 80 and 100 hours to build up the natural ash glazes. At 1200°C, the clay is hot enough for the ash fallout from the flame to melt onto the clay surfaces. Lush natural ash glazes form high in the kiln, whilst coral-like aggregates form in the firebox.

Barbara also uses slabs for an ongoing series of work, which is again inspired by her experience of the landscape of Eastern Australia. The method used in making these pieces involves

Like the First Dewfall *by Barbara Campbell-Allen, 2004. Porcelain, stoneware and earthenware clays, natural ash glaze, 31.5 x 39 x 9cm.*

PHOTOGRAPH BY MICHEL BROUET. © THE ARTIST

combining coils of different clays, including earthenware, stoneware and porcelain.

Having been formed by a combination of squeezing and rolling, the coils are placed together, joined and then rolled out with a rolling pin to form a slab. Using a rectangular board as a template, the slab is cut to the required shape. The edges are then folded back and the slab is turned over to rest on the folded edges. Like all Barbara's work, this series of slab pieces was developed with an understanding of possible effects when fired in specific areas of the anagama, in this instance, the firebox, as

she explains: 'Complex surfaces result from contrasting clays and how they respond to their firing location. Intermingled clays shrink at different rates to rip apart, twist or marry during the long anagama firing.'

These slabs, with their richly coloured and textured surfaces, speak of geological formations and the effects of the elements over millennia. They confirm detailed exploration of landscape and an attachment to it. But they also reveal the story of their making and days of intense heat and direct stoking in the anagama firebox.

Barbara concludes: 'I utilize the possibilities of the anagama process in exploring my experience of land. The anagama process, because of its nature of uncertainty, echoes my response to the experience of various environments.'

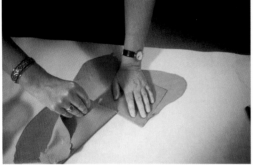 

Trudy Ellen Golley rolling out a thin slab of clay, using wooden slats as a guide to thickness. Paper-like sheets are torn from the stretched thin slabs of clay, using a cardboard template.

The centre section is cut from the stack of slabs. The top slab, which is made from three or four paper-thin layers, is attached to the walls.

PHOTOGRAPHS BY PAUL LEATHERS

TRUDY ELLEN GOLLEY

Trudy Ellen Golley is a Canadian artist who works in a variety of media, frequently combining different materials in a single sculpture or installation. She mainly uses clay however, often employing the technique of slab-building to construct individual pieces. Other processes used in her clay-based work are press-moulding and slip-casting. For example, large free-standing ceramic figures are built by slab, with press-moulded and slip-cast additions and components.

The themes that reoccur in Trudy's work concern feminine experience and exploration of her identity as a woman artist – her personal creative journey. In recent pieces she has addressed the subject of fairytales, in particular investigating gender stereotyping in contemporary tellings of fairytales compared with earlier, original versions. Trudy says of her work: 'I endeavour to explore and explain the world to myself through the creation of physical objects informed by personal experience. I question the social constructs that have formed and continue to influence me by observing gender stereotypes and the various ways in which they are promoted, ultimately using them as the raw material in a continuing narrative.'

A technique that Trudy has used recently,

both in her installations and individual sculptures, involves stacking very thin, square-shaped, sheets of clay to create paper stacks.

First a base is formed to support the clay sheets while the piece is being built. This consists of a clay form that is made slightly convex and irregular so as to encourage the bottom edges of the clay sheets to turn up asymmetrically. The centre of the support base is cut out to accommodate the foot ring on which the stack will stand. After the base has been allowed to harden, a sheet of plastic is placed on top to prevent the stack from sticking to it. A circular foot ring is then placed within the cavity of the support and trimmed to size so

Memory Pillow *by Trudy Ellen Golley (Canada), 2003. Mid-range stoneware, glazed, 24K gold lustre, sandblasted, 7 x 13.5 x 13.5cm.*

PHOTOGRAPH BY PAUL LEATHERS. © THE ARTIST

that it is level with it. To make the layers for the 'stack', fine white stoneware is rolled out to a thickness of 6mm (0.2in). These slabs are then stretched on a smooth work surface until they are paper-thin. Using a cardboard template, paper-like sheets of clay are torn from the slabs. The first, or bottom sheet, is placed on the hardened support and joined to the foot ring. Then further sheets are stacked on top of it, with casting slip (made from the same clay body) used to join them. Approximately six sheets are used to make the base layer of the stack. Subsequent sheets are only slipped close to their edges, as layers are built up until the desired wall height is reached. A square centre section is then removed from the stack to create a hollow form. Three to four thin sheets are joined together with slip to make the top layer and are attached to the walls of the stack form. In some instances, if the stack is to support an object in the completed sculpture, it is pressed into the top of the stack at this stage, using a thin piece of foam to protect the delicate surface of the clay. The paper-like clay layers are still very wet and malleable, and are easily deformed to give the impression of weight and fragility. Once the clay is firm enough to support its own weight on the foot ring base, the support is removed, and the plastic separator is peeled off. The stack is now complete and allowed to dry fully.

One of the sculptures that Trudy made using this technique is a piece with the title *Memory Pillow*. Once dry, the paper stack was fired to cone 2 (1160°C) to harden the clay, but not completely vitrify it. A transparent turquoise glaze was applied to the top layer and a thin wash of a cryolite/soda ash glaze was applied to the rest of the stack. The piece was then fired to cone 04 (1060°C). Next, a sandblasting mask out was applied to the surface of the top layer and the silhouette of the peony was sandblasted, leaving the flower and border with the glossy turquoise surface. Trudy then worked back into the gloss area using white gouache (which is very high in kaolin) as a lustre resist to create brush marks, and applied 24K gold lustre over the whole surface. The piece was then fired to cone 018 (717°C). After this third firing, a soft cloth was used to polish off the gouache, revealing the shiny glaze as brushstrokes against the glossy gold. The gold takes on the surface quality of whatever it is applied to, resulting in areas of gold over the glaze, and matt gold/purple metallic over the vitrified bare clay.

Trudy explains that *Memory Pillow* grew from the challenge of being invited to participate in a theme exhibition in Hong Kong and Shanghai, entitled 'To Dream the Impossible'.

> I worked to marry the notion of the Chinese ceramic pillow form with references from my own work. As a result of the struggle, I found that my research led me to investigate Sung Dynasty pillows and the imagery that they carried. *Memory Pillow* gathers in the idea of unwritten histories – women's stories in particular – and glosses these over with the beautiful peony motif that, according to my research, is the symbol for a happy life and good marriage.

Some of Trudy's sculptures incorporate the use of light. In a wall piece with the title *Listen to...* reflected light is an important element in the effect created by the overall work. 'New works like *Listen to...* are made with the idea that they will be placed in an interior and will come to life when lit. In each circumstance and with different lighting, the work will create a unique aurora personalized to the individual setting.'

Like much of Trudy's work, this piece is made from white stoneware clay, reinforced with cellulose fibre. The paper content is very low, about one per cent by volume, so as to exploit the quality of the cellulose while retaining the working qualities of regular clay. The addition of the cellulose fibre allows for more extreme handling during construction of the work, with less cracking and warping. Ironically, Trudy does not use cellulose-rein-

Listen to... by Trudy Ellen Golley, 2004.
Slab-built stoneware wall piece, glaze and 24K gold lustre, 37 x 37 x 15cm.

PHOTOGRAPH BY PAUL LEATHERS. © THE ARTIST

forced clay (paper clay) for her 'paper stack' forms, as the fibre prevents the clay from stretching in the manner required for these particular pieces.

'*Listen to...* is a response to the seemingly endless Canadian winters.' Trudy adds:

> The coldest afternoons in Alberta are most often filled with bright sunshine, wind-sculpted snow formations, and at dusk, long purple shadows. The nights are clear, fresh, and star-filled and occasionally punctuated by the magic of the aurora borealis (northern lights).

When this piece is placed on a wall, the dazzling, lustrous, gold-lined surface of the softened spiral-shaped gouge casts a light onto the surrounding area that is reminiscent of the cold winter sunlight that inspired the work. But depending on lighting conditions, one imagines that a wondrous array of colours would instead be seen.

Trudy says of the inspiration for the series of work that includes *Listen to...*:

> Over the course of my studio practice, I have used light to attract and locate the viewer, to provide an unexpected sense of discovery and to address notions of conceptual and intellectual illumination. I construct ceramic forms that capture, transmit, obstruct and redirect light in order to exploit its qualities in an ongoing exploration of material and vision. Pieces, such as *Listen to...* explore the material and immaterial through the creation of a drawing in light and shadow. Interested in how elements such as fired clay, glass and gold may be brought into conjunction with each other, I create novel forms and experiences for the viewer to encounter. Without depicting a specific event, object or place, I aim to capture a sense of the sublime in order to hold the viewer's attention and trigger their imagination.

FRANCES PRIEST

Frances Priest's abstract ceramic forms have a presence and monumentality that deny their actual scale. They are built from curved, pale-coloured slabs of clay, and, on viewing these sculptural structures from different angles, one is immediately aware of inner and outer planes, precise angles, crisp edges and subtle variations of light and shade that prompt further exploration. The sensitive use of line, texture and colour and the balance of surface markings with form richly reward our closer attention.

While still at art college, Frances, who is based in the United Kingdom, developed a method of working with bone china, casting very thin sheets that were subsequently 'kiln formed' over setters during firing. Bone china was made into a casting slip, to which a very fine paper pulp was added, the paper serving the same purpose as it does in paper clay, its fibres holding the clay body together. The addition of the paper pulp gave added strength in the green state, making it possible to cast very thin slabs that were stronger and consequently more manageable. To achieve precise shapes, Frances used rulers, set squares and scalpel blades, working with the sheets of clay as though they were cardboard. These shapes were then laid over setters (which had been coated in bat wash and alumina) and fired to just below 1260°C. The temperature was critical, as the forms would lose their crisp edges and go out of shape if over-fired even slightly. The setters were made from an industrial insulating castable (a concrete-type material that could withstand repeated high firings) in clay or wooden moulds.

Frances comments on the work that she made at this time:

> I think this early work was looking mainly at process and material – creating an object that would highlight or capture the moment of

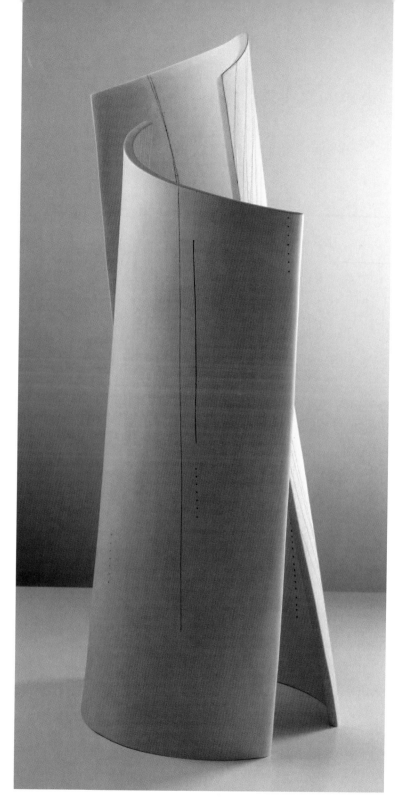

Untitled (Tall Double Curve Series, I) *by Frances Priest (UK), 2003. Porcelain/stoneware mix.*

PHOTOGRAPH BY
SHANNON TOFTS. © THE ARTIST

Untitled (Bone China Form) *by Frances Priest,*
2000. 20 x 33 x 31cm.

PHOTOGRAPH BY LISA PRENDERGAST. © THE ARTIST

change that occurs during the firing process
at the point of vitrification. The objects themselves looked like they were made of paper and
the outer edges appeared to me like lines in
space. This work led on to an interest in defin-
ing positive and negative space. I liked the
fragile state of the objects, the uncertainty
over the material – paper/ceramic – and the
sense of movement in the later curved pieces,
making the work seem unstable and tense.

Frances continued working in bone china for
some years. However, in 2002, when preparing
for her first solo exhibition, she chose to change
material and began using instead a body made
from a combination of white stoneware (containing a high proportion of Molochite) and
porcelain. Her reasons for this change were

that the focus of her work had moved towards
the relationship between form and surface
drawing, and she needed a material that would
facilitate this. The porcelain gave the body a
slightly lighter and creamier/white appearance, making a suitable canvas for surface line
drawings. Frances also wanted to increase the
scale of her work and have more freedom over
the forms that she was building. She explains:
'Using bone china was becoming more about
mastery of a process than using the material to
explore ideas – the balance was wrong.'

In creating work from the combined porcelain and stoneware body, large slabs were
banged down onto sheets of fabric and
stretched to the required thickness. The slabs
were then laid over various wooden formers
and, when they were sufficiently firm to support their own weight, the forms were made
through a 'reductive process' by paring, using
knives, metal kidneys and surforms. Once the
form was 'found', marks were drawn onto the

Shifting Grid *by Frances Priest, 2005.*
Stoneware, slip inlay and glaze,
47 x 43 x 6cm.

Shifting Grid *(detail) by Frances Priest,*
2005. Stoneware, slip inlay and glaze.

PHOTOGRAPH BY SHANNON TOFTS. © THE ARTIST

surface using a variety of knives, and the cuts inlaid with black and grey slips. The work was low fired to around 900°C, polished using diamond pads and then re-fired to around 1130°C. Following this second firing, the pieces were polished again. At this stage further lines were sometimes added using transfers. Drawings were made into transfers, cut up and applied to the clay surface, or solid sheets

of black and white were printed, which were cut into narrow strips for application as lines. The use of these transfers created a subtle difference in line quality.

Describing the concerns she was addressing in the forms created during this period, Frances wrote:

My work explores the relationship between surface and form using mark making as a means of highlighting the boundaries and relationships that exist between two and three dimensions. The clay acts as both a canvas and as a means of creating forms that cut through or contain space, almost as three-dimensional drawings. The strong architectural structures of the forms are contrasted by the more delicate fragile lines that pin down the surfaces; at points in harmony with the form, at others in discord, creating a dynamic set of relationships between volume and plane.

She continued: 'The forms are universal, referencing geometry, the golden section, architecture, but the point was to achieve almost a universal form, a sense of rightness. By pairing forms I wanted to create a sense of tension or imminent change.'

Recent work has again involved a change in material, and is made from the same white stoneware clay, now without the addition of porcelain, which results in a fired body colour that is not quite as light or creamy. However, there is far more use of pattern, surface drawing and colour in the new work. The method used to create the slab forms is the same, and inlay techniques are still used, but in addition to slip, glaze is sometimes inlaid into cut lines, adding 'a richer, more luscious quality to the colour and creating an interesting contrast with the drier, flatter slip'. Surface marks are also applied using slip, sometimes a whole area is covered in a solid colour, and at other times stencils are used in applying a repeating pattern.

Of her ongoing work Frances says:

> The exploration of the boundaries between two and three dimensions continues. Shape is a construct that is difficult to define, sitting perfectly on the boundary between two and three dimensions, it is neither flat nor fully formed. The objects I create are, I think, decorative, and are unashamedly so. They are the distillation of the things I see and respond to in the world.

NINA HOLE

Nina Hole is a Danish sculptor who produces large outdoor ceramic works, as well as smaller-scale pieces intended for interior settings. Both categories of work have clay slabs as their basis. For more than ten years, Nina has been constructing large 'fire sculptures' – unique pieces in which the 'kiln' that fires the work is an integral part of the sculpture itself.

Before Nina began this phase of her work, she had used slab-building as the method of forming relatively small-scale sculptures, as she explains:

> I have favoured building with slabs almost since the beginning of my work in clay. I have long been interested in the built environment and my forms and ideas are inspired by architecture, ranging from ancient structures to the most modern buildings around the world. These ideas lend themselves to being built by slab construction. It seems to me to be the most direct method to accomplish building and construction systems.

Some of Nina's small sculptures are low fired in an oxidizing atmosphere (to 1030°C) and are glazed in bright, low temperature glazes, while others are wood-fired and have more subtle tones and fired effects resulting from high temperature woodfiring. In these sculptures there are obvious references to architectural forms, predominantly houses and the traditional churches of Nina's native Denmark. Often the sculptures can be 'turned upside-down' so that the structure is seen as a series of interconnecting vessel forms.

With regard to her method for making the initial slabs from which her small sculptures are formed, Nina explains:

> I prefer to throw the slabs on the floor, and for this reason I have a cement floor in my studio.

Folded Architecture *by Nina Hole (Denmark).*
Wood-fired, 43 x 46 x 23cm. © THE ARTIST

It absorbs some moisture from the clay, and in this way releases the clay slab. I much prefer this 'floor' method to using a slab roller. In working in this way, firstly the clay gets wedged, and the slabs become much stronger and more flexible, and secondly, I can throw the clay out into whichever shape I want to work with. It was Richard Zakin [US potter] who introduced me to this method of forming slabs.

Nina's large pieces – her fire sculptures – developed from a desire to create large outdoor work without the constraints of kiln size, or indeed, location. After much experimentation she came up with the idea of combining the kiln and sculpture in a single form, the firebox of the kiln becoming the brick base of the finished work, and the sculpture, by supporting and being wrapped in ceramic fibre blanket, would be the 'kiln', with its own internal chimney. The most important question, however, was how to

A long narrow clay slab being extruded in readiness for making the modules from which Nina Hole's fire sculptures are constructed.

ABOVE: *The 'J' shaped modules drying.*

RIGHT: *Work in progress on a fire sculpture, showing modules in position.*

construct the sculpture so that it would both facilitate and withstand this method of firing.

Nina goes on to describe how she resolved this problem:

My earlier work in slabs led me directly to developing the slab module system that I have been using for my fire sculptures. The module is a slab piece folded into a 'J' shape. Alternate rows are turned in opposite directions, and in this way the modules form a double wall, with an 'O' shaped gap running all the way up through the structure. I was looking for a technique that would allow me to work with the clay in the fastest, strongest and most direct way, and also a module system that was so open in its construction that it would allow for fast drying, fast firing, and would be capable of withstanding the shock of fast cooling.

35

OPPOSITE:
Firing A House for Everyone, *fire sculpture by Nina Hole.*

RIGHT: A House for Everyone, *fire sculpture by Nina Hole, 2005. Height 3.5m, glazed. Constructed and fired to cone 02 on site in Kecskemét, Hungary. Commissioned by The International Ceramics Centre, Kecskemét.*

Since 1995 Nina has created fire sculptures in many locations around the world, including the USA, Taiwan, Wales, Australia, Canada, Sweden, Portugal, Hungary, Lithuania, Denmark and Greece. The tallest of these, at more than 4m (12ft) in height, was the monumental *Commemorative H*, built in 2002 in the grounds of the School of Fine Arts in Athens, Greece, on the occasion of the 50th Anniversary meeting of the International Academy of Ceramics. It was a collaboration between Nina and Fred Olsen (US potter and kiln/firing expert). Working with a team of assistants, this piece took a week to construct, using more than two and a half tons of clay, and some 72 hours to fire.

Nina explains that 'the first four or five fire sculptures were constructed from "hand-thrown" slabs'. She continues:

> Later, Fred Olsen, with whom I have worked on several fire sculptures, made an extruder for me, and since then it has been a great help to extrude the slabs. It also makes the slabs uniform, and enables each new assistant to join in the work process quickly. However, in a recent fire sculpture, in Fredonia, New York, USA, the clay could not be extruded, so a slab roller was taken over for the production.

On some occasions, Nina adds between twenty-five and thirty per cent of paper pulp to the clay used for making her fire sculptures, for strength at the green stage and also to make it lighter. Once construction of the sculpture has been completed, terra sigillata, oxides and glaze are applied to the exterior surface, depending on the sculpture and where it is placed. Sometimes small paper packets containing a mixture of salt and sulphates are placed within some of the apertures in the sculpture. The form is then wrapped in layers of ceramic fibre blanket, using thin metal wire and nails to hold it in place. The scaffolding and other support structures that were used during the construction of the sculpture are then removed.

The sculptures are constructed on top of a firebrick structure designed to serve as either two or four cross-draught fireboxes. The firing begins with small fires in all the fireboxes. Depending on the drying/weather conditions and time scale for completion of the work, these fires are sometimes lit while work continues to complete the upper section of the sculpture. (If it is possible, gas is used to preheat/dry out the sculpture before the firing proper begins.) The fires are gradually increased in size. The gaps, which are a feature in the construction of the sculpture, allow the flames and heat to permeate up through it. At the very top of the structure, two pieces of fibre blanket, acting as a damper, are left loose for controlling the draught and allowing the opportunity to move them if it is necessary to keep the top almost closed so as to create a down-draught to even out the temperature. When the required temperature has been reached (varying from 1000°C to 1200°C, depending on the clay used), usually after two or three days and nights of firing, the ceramic fibre is removed – always at night, spectacularly revealing the glowing sculpture beneath. At this stage observers of the spectacle are invited to participate by throwing sawdust onto the clay surface – sending showers of sparks skywards in a dramatic pyrotechnic display.

While there is certainly a strong element of performance involved in Nina's fire sculptures, particularly at the exciting moment when the fibre blanket is removed at top temperature, this is only one aspect of their creation. In the period leading up to the construction of each work, Nina gives very careful consideration to its design and location. Preparatory drawings are made, and considerable time is spent figuring out the technical logistics of creating, and especially firing such large-scale works, which are almost always sited in locations with public

LEFT: *Conrad Snider 'hand-pounds' a block of clay into a basic tile shape. Placing a textured rubber mould on the tile.*

ABOVE: *Having placed the tile-shaped block on a concrete floor covered in grog, it is cut to the required shape and size using a wooden template.*

access. Then there is all the practical preparation carried out by Nina, and usually a group of several helpers, of extruding the long narrow slabs and forming them into the building modules; ensuring that there is sufficient dry wood for the firing; erecting scaffolding to facilitate work on the upper areas of the structure as it increases in height. There is also the construction process itself – a very intensive period of work, which usually takes place within a strictly limited time scale.

Nina's fire sculptures are site specific and remain in the place where they were both created and fired, a feature that distinguishes them from much contemporary large-scale ceramic sculpture.

When Nina was asked what the biggest challenge was for her in her work, she responded: 'It is to push the boundaries that I know – just go a little beyond what I did before, that is the challenge to test myself.'

CONRAD SNIDER

Conrad Snider works on a massive scale. At his 1115 square metre (12000sq ft) studio in Kansas, USA, he produces work for architectural settings, both outdoor and interior, including tile murals and large, free-standing forms that are either figurative or vessel based. Both categories of work begin in the same manner – with the making of what Conrad describes as 'hand-pounded' tiles and slabs.

Much of Conrad's work is commissioned by public institutions for installation in buildings such as libraries, banks and churches, and he also collaborates with other artists in joint public art projects. Text is often inscribed on the surface of his work, thus, as Conrad explains, 'allowing the viewer to identify with the pieces on many different levels'. In some instances, the text is illegible, its purpose being to add texture to the clay surface.

A large ball of wadding, placed in the centre, and eight small marbles made from unglazed high-fired porcelain are used when packing tiles in the kiln for biscuit firing.

Concerning both his sculptural forms and murals Conrad explains:

All these forms as single pieces of clay are restricted by the scale limitations of the kilns. Although the figures are essentially human scaled, approximately six feet tall and the vessels range from six to eight feet, a desire to push scale farther has led me to also make tile murals. The modular format of these murals naturally allows for a much larger piece, bringing the viewer into more of an architectural frame of mind. Smooth hand-pounded tiles emphasize the two-dimensional painterly aspects of murals. Other tiles, being thicker, sometimes three to four inches thick, allow for a more sculptural use of the material, while maintaining the modular characteristics of the mural format.

Conrad uses a stoneware clay body that is heavily grogged. After the clay has been mixed, it is stacked in a 680kg (1500lb) mound, from which amounts are taken as required for making either tiles or slabs. The clay is wedged, and then pounded and turned over five or six times, to compress and strengthen it, as it is shaped to the size and thickness required.

The surfaces of some tiles are textured using a rubber mould. The mould is placed on top of the pounded tile, and they are turned over so that the tile lies face down on the mould. The back of the tile is hand-pounded to ensure that the texture from the mould is clearly imparted onto the front surface. The back is scored in readiness for installation, the scoring also helping to prevent warping. A board is placed on top of the tile, which is then turned the right way up, with the rubber mould still in place.

At this stage the tiles are laid on a concrete floor sprinkled with a layer of grog. The concrete aids in even drying, and the grog allows the tile to move as it shrinks. The rubber mould is then peeled away, and, with a board template placed on top, the tile is cut to size. Conrad stresses that he supports the corners of the tile as he cuts to prevent stressing the clay, which would cause it to warp. Once the tiles have dried to the leatherhard stage, the cut edges are scraped gently to smooth them. They are then allowed to dry for a few weeks before being bisque fired.

When stacking tiles in the kiln, a space is left under each one, allowing for even heating of the top and bottom, to help prevent warping. First, a 2.5cm (1in) ball of wadding is placed on the kiln shelf so that it will be directly underneath the centre of the tile. Then eight 1.3cm (0.5in) sized marbles made of unglazed high-fired porcelain are placed around the centre wadding. These marbles allow the tiles to shrink as they are fired, while still being supported. When the tile is put in position on the kiln shelf, the centre wadding flattens out, keeping the tile in place. In bisque firings a second tile is stacked on top of the first, using nine wads to support it evenly, as well as allowing space between the tiles. After the biscuit

ABOVE: **Handmade Ceramic Tile Mural** *by Conrad Snider (USA). Stoneware, reduction fired, 182 x 305cm.*

PHOTOGRAPH BY VADA SNIDER. © THE ARTIST

RIGHT: *Conrad Snider adding a slab to a vessel form.*

firing the tiles are glazed. The first layer of glaze is usually poured on, with additional layers sprayed on (using a garden pump sprayer) to create colour and texture variations. The tiles are then reduction fired to cone 10 in a natural gas-fired kiln.

The clay used in making both handbuilt and wheel-thrown forms is hand-pounded into long blocks or slabs. The handbuilt forms usually consist of two or three separate sections, which are built one on top on of the other. When in place, the first layer of slabs is allowed to stiffen (sometimes for a day or two) before

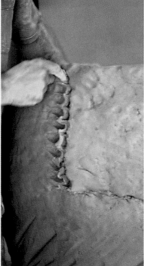

ABOVE: *Joining the slabs of a large vessel form. Clay is pushed across the join from one side to the other, and the process is repeated in the opposite direction along the full length of the join. The same procedure is carried out both on the inside and outside of the form.*

LEFT: *The vessel form nearing completion.*

PHOTOGRAPHS BY HANNA EASTIN

the top edge is scored and sprayed and the next layer of slabs added.

As Conrad constructs the lower section, he stacks concrete blocks within the form that will support the weight of the next section as it is constructed. Once the first section is complete, but whilst it is still damp, its top rim is measured and a plywood bat cut to the same size. Two 2cm (0.8in) rings are then cut from the bat's circumference. These rings or bands (each in two semicircular pieces) are subsequently screwed back onto the bat. When the lower section of the form is relatively dry and has shrunk to size, the ringed bat is placed on the concrete block support and construction of the upper section commences. As work progresses the clay of the upper section is allowed to slump down over the edge of the plywood bat and follow the form of the lower section. (This creates a more natural join and also ensures that the two sections will fit together well when they are assembled after firing.)

Once the clay of the upper section stiffens and begins to dry, the two plywood rings are removed from the bat, allowing the clay to shrink whilst it is still being supported on the bat. (The screws holding the rings in place are inserted at an angle from underneath, using a screw gun with an extension tip. When the bands are unscrewed the parts can be removed through the gap between the upper and lower sections of the form. The profile of the upper section of the form can then be aligned with that of the lower one, uninterrupted by the bat.)

When work has been completed, the forms are allowed to dry, in some cases for up to a year. They are then bisque fired, the firing lasting for up to three weeks. The first part of this firing is controlled manually and is then transferred to a computer program. Two natural gas-fired kilns, a down-draught (1.4 x 1.5 x 1.15m/4.6 x 5 x 3.8ft) and a cylindrical up-draught (2 x 0.9m/6.6 x 3ft) are used for both biscuit and glaze firings. In glaze firings the computer controls the firing up to reduction temperature, Conrad then manually sets the reduction and fires to a top temperature of cone 10.

With regard to the inspiration for his work, Conrad comments:

All of us inhabit a certain space, drawing our sense of self-worth and understanding of the world from our relation to the objects and individuals that also inhabit that space. The majority of my work explores that set of relationships with large-scale objects. These range from traditional pottery forms such as vessels, teapots, jars and platters, to figurative work,

One-of-a-Kind, Large-scale Ceramic Vessel (#204-03) *by Conrad Snider.*
Stoneware, reduction fired, height 175cm, diameter 73.5cm.
PHOTOGRAPH BY VADA SNIDER. © THE ARTIST

utilizing a form we are all quite familiar with, but do not fully understand.

The use of traditional, pottery-related forms lends a connection to a much larger history of clay and its almost universal connection with human culture throughout the world, currently and historically. While drawing from the ideas of the pottery forms, exaggerated scale removes the idea of function as part of their definition, replacing it with an altered sense of how we relate to these types of objects.

SARAH WALTON

Sarah Walton has been producing salt-glazed ceramics at her studio in East Sussex, England, since 1975. Her early functional work, which was mostly wheel thrown, was often worked on extensively afterwards. Many pieces, inspired by Greek archaic sculpture, were carved and incised, creating richly textured surfaces that were subtly accentuated by salt-glazing.

A desire to work more instinctively led to a change in the direction of Sarah's work in 1985. It became larger in scale and more

Birdbath by Sarah Walton (UK). Salt-glazed stoneware, 20 x 38 x 38cm. Wood base, 38 x 30 x 30cm.

'The 'V' shape in one side of the birdbath was prompted by a dramatic crack, first seen by chance in a wood base. I decided I'd use it in the design of the piece. When no more lengths of wood base with cracks in them could be found, I started to have 'V's cut out intentionally.'

PHOTOGRAPH BY ORNAN ROTEM. © THE ARTIST

Birdbath *by Sarah Walton. Salt-glazed stoneware, 23 x 46 x 42cm. Wood base, 45 x 30 x 30cm.*

PHOTOGRAPH BY ORNAN ROTEM. © THE ARTIST

sculptural in form as she began making forms intended for placing outdoors, particularly in garden settings. These are her birdbath forms, which she has evolved slowly during the past twenty years.

Landscape is a dominant theme in Sarah's work, having, as she says: 'walked, drawn and painted it since childhood'. She adds: 'When I came to evolve my birdbaths, I drew on those years of walking, of feeling the landscape under my feet, leaning into hills as I climbed them, seeing tarns gleaming through mist and the exhilaration at the end of hours of hiking.' She is also drawn to the qualities inherent in materials such as stone and wood, which have been softened and eroded over time by use or weather conditions. In this context, one of her sources of inspiration is the stone staircase leading to the chapter house in Wells Cathedral.

There was much experimenting with processes before Sarah eventually found a satisfactory technique for constructing the forms. The first birdbaths were made as solid forms that were hollowed out. These then became coiled double-walled forms, with supporting internal walls. At one point, she tried subdividing the forms into two, four and then eight sections, which were assembled using a resin putty. Eventually, Sarah resolved many of the technical problems and began using press moulds to slab-build the forms. Five repeatable shapes of birdbaths are currently produced. She now uses what she describes as 'more precise' two- or three-piece press moulds. Slabs of clay, which have been rolled out to a thickness of approximately 2cm (0.8in) on canvas, are pressed into the moulds and allowed to stiffen. Later on these sections are removed from their moulds and joined together. As with the making process, the present clay body is the result of trial and error, and Sarah now has it made up to her recipe in Stoke-on-Trent.

A hand-operated mobile hoist is used for lifting the pieces at every stage of making. A wooden pallet is laid over the horizontal platform of the hoist, and the moulds with clay stiffening in them – and later the assembled birdbaths – stand on these pallets. Both hoist and pallets are essential equipment in the making of this work. When they are fully dry (a dehumidifier having been used during this period), the birdbaths are biscuit fired to 850°C.

Sarah uses very few, if any, slips on the surfaces of the birdbaths, as she explains:

A lot of my birdbaths have no coating at all – it's just bare clay, no dressing or colour, just dependent on the clay body, the effects of the salt and the way I fire the kiln. I know the range of possibilities, but I don't know, until I open the kiln, what will happen. Pots for domestic use can be more decorative and colourful, but the birdbaths must work with 'the outside'.

She continues:

I didn't think that I would be using salt-glaze this long. It is a temperamental, uncontrollable, wild, natural method. But it still excites me. I have looked at what happens to the wall of the kiln and thought that the qualities are so thrilling. And I have thought, 'Can I not simplify the forms, and let them then just be the vehicle for the flames and heat?' It is like someone working with the grain of wood. I work with the path of the flames across my work, knowing that all sorts of subtle things will happen in the kiln and, in a way, trying to leave room for that.

The kiln used for salt-glazing has a $1.13m^3$ (40ft³) stacking space. It is oil fired and is Sarah's original kiln, built in 1975. Firings last thirty-nine hours. After firing, the entire surface of the forms is worked with Carborundum 'wet and dry' paper.

All the birdbaths have wooden bases, sections cut from lengths of 30 x 30cm (12 x 12in) recycled Dockland timber. (Local green oak will soon be used instead.) In considering the bases for the forms, Sarah stresses that at all costs she 'wants to avoid the appearance of a mushroom on a stalk. The birdbath mustn't be too much wider than its base. In fact, base and birdbath should be seen as two parts of one whole rather than a piece sitting on a pedestal.'

With this work, Sarah aims at 'getting form and content to serve one another.' She continues:

I have always thought 'understatement' is important to me, but I also know I am after something rich as well as powerful. The urge to find a personal note is strong. Finding the birdbaths involved allowing myself to make a new start, using as my guide the things that interested me.

DAVID MILLER

David Miller's studio is in the Languedoc-Roussillon region of the south of France, where he has lived since 1980, having moved there from England. For many years he produced a range of brightly coloured, slip-decorated functional work, including large slab dishes. These dishes were a suitable vehicle for the lively and colourful surfaces that David created by brushing and trailing areas of coloured slips onto a background of white slip.

From the early 1990s, David extended his range of forms to include pieces in which function was not the major priority. At this time he also built a woodfire kiln for firing this work, as he wanted to achieve a glazed surface that was different from the very glossy glazes of his functional pots, which were fired in an electric kiln. David has continued to develop this range of work, which includes slab wall pieces.

In making the slabs for these pieces, David uses a method that he considers to be far easier than rolling them out. Separate lengths

David Miller applying white slip to a wall piece using a paint roller.

Successive layers of coloured slips are built up on the surface of a wall piece using paint rollers, brushes and slip trailers.

PHOTOGRAPHS BY DOMINIQUE FORCES

ABOVE: *Detail of* Wall Piece *by David Miller.*

LEFT: **Wall Piece** *by David Miller*
(UK/France). Earthenware, coloured slips,
wood-fired.

PHOTOGRAPHS BY DAVID MILLER. © THE ARTIST

of wood are screwed down to a blockwood base, creating a frame of the shape, size and depth to form the required slab. Curved shapes are formed by using thin pieces of laminate or hardboard, bent around wooden blocks, which are nailed or screwed to the base board. Grog is sprinkled onto the blockwood base and then very soft red earthenware clay is slopped into the frame, a method of fabrication that resembles ancient brick-making techniques. The clay

Wall Piece *by David Miller. Earthenware, coloured slips, wood-fired.*

is compressed by tamping down the board that the frame is attached to. Excess clay is removed and the surface levelled using a straight-edged metal bar.

The clay slab is allowed to dry slowly until it is stiff enough to hold its shape once the wooden frame is removed. The edges of the slab are then tidied up and when it has dried to leather-hard, an even coating of white slip is applied to the top surface in several layers, using a paint roller. Once this has dried, areas of coloured slips are applied using brushes, trailers or smaller paint rollers. These coloured slips are made by mixing commercial stains with the basic white slip.

One of the methods of applying coloured slips that David uses is to put slip of one colour onto a small paint roller, then shapes such as dots of another colour of slip are put on top. When rolled on the slab, the images are transferred to the surface.

In the decoration of David's functional work, there was initially a strong Mediterranean influence of intense colour, depicting fruit, vegetables, eating and wine. Gradually, the areas of colour became increasingly abstract. On his wall pieces, layers of colour and marks made on the surface by scratching through the slip to reveal the clay body underneath combine to create richly coloured and

49

textured surfaces. The overall affect is spontaneous and painterly.

Drawing plays an important role throughout David's creative process. Initially, line
drawings are made of the forms that he wants
to create, before considering the most suitable
method for making them. This is a process he
enjoys, developing new techniques to solve
technical problems. In working on the clay surface, he draws using fine-tipped slip trailers,
often outlining areas of colour with thin black
trailed lines. David explains that: 'No preparatory drawings are made before this drawing-
painting stage. The process is different from
that of the functional pieces in that the marks
made on the surface can be erased, changed,
modified at will.'

On some pieces, additional triangular
shapes made separately are attached to the
main slab. The wall pieces are biscuit fired to a
temperature of 1000°C in an electric kiln. A
thin layer of lead bisilicate glaze is then applied.
The pieces are packed in the kiln for the glaze
firing, stood on edge and supported by large triangular porcelain stilts.

Sometimes these stilts sink into the body of
the piece, creating interesting combinations,
and can be ground down to create a white tri-
angle. The 2m³ (70ft³) up-draught, woodfire
kiln is fired to a temperature of over 1100°C.
David explains that this type of kiln is more
often fired to temperatures of no higher than
1000°C, and taking it the last 100 degrees to
the higher temperature is particularly labori-
ous. However, he considers that 'the smoke and
flame help to achieve interesting modifications
to the colour and marks' on his wall pieces.

David's ideas for future development in-
volve 'using woodfire to bring together form,
clay-making techniques, the mark-making
phase, colour and the heat flame-firing part,
so that "form and decoration" become one –
an amalgam'.

JOHN GLICK

John Glick has been a potter since 1964. At his
studio in Michigan, USA, he produces a wide
range of work, much of it wheel-thrown functional ware, with many pieces altered both during and after throwing. John sets part of each
working session aside for producing large, one-
of-a-kind dinner sets that are made on a com-
mission basis. A range of work is also made
from extruded clay sections, which, increasingly, are combined with thrown parts.

Devising and making specialist tools to be
used in creating specific pots, or components of
pots, has been an important aspect of John's
work. Since the late 1970s he has made extensive use of the extruder as a creative design tool
in making clay sections which are then constructed into forms such as lidded boxes, large
serving trays and planters.

Having previously handbuilt slab pots using
various techniques and processes including
moulds made from plaster, biscuit fired clay
and wood, he found that, to varying degrees,
all displayed evidence of the stresses that the
slab walls underwent in the forming process,
and particularly during the high-temperature
firing. It was for this reason that he decided to
try using an extruder to create components for
the pots that he wanted to make.

Initially, John used a commercially manu-
factured extruder that had a 10cm (4in) barrel.
Then, wanting to form larger-sized extrusions,
he proceeded to make an extruder with a 15cm
(6in) barrel, followed by other, larger versions.

Pots formed from extruded components
proved to be far more stable during firing than
those made from rolled slabs. However, John
stresses that to achieve this stability, care must
be taken at all stages, including during the
extrusion process itself, and subsequent handling of the clay sections when the form is
being assembled. The choice of clay is also very
important for a successful outcome. John has

found that for his purposes the most suitable clay is a 'well aged, very plastic, fine-grained body of medium-stiff consistency'.

His method of working is that he first of all makes detailed drawings of the type of pot that he wants to create. Next, he considers the most appropriate method of forming it, and the shapes of the separate components that will be required to construct it. He then designs and makes the dies that will be required to extrude these sections.

Extruded clay pieces gradually became more complex, and over the years John has made hundreds of dies for producing clay elements for his range of constructed ceramic forms. Most of these dies are made from good grade marine veneer plywood, acrylic, or, in some instances, steel or aluminium, when extra strength is required. John explains that this collection of extruder dies has included 'smaller

Wall panel, Landscape Series, *by John Glick (USA), 1994. Stoneware with slips, oxide washes and glazes; multiple firings to cone 10, reduction; 58 x 66 x 5cm. Extruded hollow slab construction.*

PHOTOGRAPH BY JOHN GLICK. © THE ARTIST

"bridging dies" made from steel and simple hardware from the supply bins at my local hardware store. Some are merely steel nails welded onto reworked, large-scale steel washers to form a die for making hollow forms.'

John works with more than sixty glazes. In his functional work, he overlays up to four glazes sequentially, often using a wax resist technique. Other decorating techniques used include dipping, pouring and brushing on glazes. In addition, glaze trailing, which is done using tiny ear syringes fitted with football inflator needles, is used extensively. Most of the

pots are fired to cone 10 in a heavily reduced atmosphere in a 2m³ (70ft³) gas-fired car kiln. There is also a 1.5m³ (55ft³) kiln for soda firing.

John Glick extruding a wide, hollow clay slab from a hydraulic extruder.
PHOTOGRAPH BY KRISTINE HOUTARI

While the majority of the work is functional, John also produces pieces in which function is not a priority, as he explains: 'I draw on the many historical precedents that give a kind of permission to move away from "pure function" occasionally, to explore other avenues in the medium.' He continues:

> A portion of my work time is devoted to making ceramic forms that are not functional in the traditional sense. My wall pieces of the early 1990s explored the realm of drawing and painting, often deriving their forms and colour from natural landscape and sky themes. Later works explored the concepts of time and nature (tree forms, leaves) and used elements from

ABOVE: *Large steel dies for the two hydraulic extruders used by John Glick. 'U' bolts, which are readily available from hardware shops, are used to assemble the bridges to make dies for extruding hollow forms.*

PHOTOGRAPH BY JOHN GLICK

OPPOSITE, BELOW: *A steel die and resulting hollow extruded elements, which were used in making a series of 'mantel-like' wall panels during the early to mid 1990s.*

PHOTOGRAPH BY JOHN GLICK

RIGHT: *John Glick assembling a wall piece from a combination of slabs and extruded components.*

PHOTOGRAPH BY PAUL YOUNG

architecture (the column) to reflect on man's impact on nature. Present works for the wall deal with personal memories and focus on a collage approach to bring together such diverse elements as mantels, fruit, pottery forms, leaves and letters into a harmonious grouping reminiscent of still life compositions.

In creating the landscape and skyscape wall panels, John's interest was to use the flat clay surface in a similar way to other surfaces for painting and drawing. The surfaces of the finished pieces are complex, with multiple applications of oxide washes, slips and glazes. Post-firing treatments involved extensive, fine detailed masking and selective sand blasting processes, which eroded the surface, removing specific layered areas of colour, thus heightening the visual effects of perspective and depth. Typically, these wall pieces measure a minimum of 60 x 60 x 5cm (24 x 24 x 2in) and are hollow in the centre.

Having explored the possibilities of colour and texture within the format of flat clay surfaces, John's work then developed into three dimensions, in the creation of a series of wall-mounted, relief sculptural compositions, the *Mantel Series*. These works were comprised of separate parts, and often included column fragments, shelves, leaves and fruit. This format was used in exploring themes such as: 'childhood memories and collections of personal treasures we have tucked away somewhere in a recess of the mind.'

Both John's wall pieces and free-standing sculptural forms are constructed using processes that were initially developed in making his functional pottery. In particular, he uses two large hydraulic powered horizontal extruders, which he built in the early 1990s. One of these has the capacity for making extrusions measuring 40cm wide, by 15cm in height (16 x 6in), while the second can produce extrusions up to 60cm wide, by 20cm

high (24 x 8in). The larger extruder requires about 68kg (150lb) of clay to fully charge the chamber. John explains: 'The logic for making sizeable equipment is not about getting into large quantities of things at all. The core reasoning is to allow me to get complex, large-scale pieces fabricated relatively quickly, so the more enjoyable aspect of forming and exploring of shapes can be more expediently realized.'

A table on wheels that can be adjusted in height was made to facilitate receiving the large, flat clay sections from these extruders. Generally, two people are required to support and manipulate the soft lengths of clay as they emerge from the die face.

The wall sculptures are constructed using a combination of slabs and extruded components. When making these forms, John usually works in series, often making up to eighteen compositions of a related family of forms. In some instances, the extrusions are altered into similar shapes in multiples, prior to being assembled to form the wall panels. John explains that: 'The logic for this approach came from wanting to make small editions of work with less fabrication time, all brought into focus through the assistance of the extrusion process.'

Eventually the wall panels and the *Mantel Series* of relief sculptures evolved into free-standing sculptures – the *Place Series*. John describes his inspiration for this series of work:

The power of 'place' to capture the imagination is what fascinates me. Having experienced the beckoning of landscapes which felt magical or meaningful, each of us can recall childhood visits to enchanted places. My ideas float in that twilight realm between memory and reality, where a 'place' can emerge . . . transformed. These small-scale sculptures are a passport to travel the landscapes we loved, the skyscapes we glimpsed, and the spirit-homes of our hearts.

John's ongoing exploration of new techniques and processes has been central in his work, both as a potter and sculptor. He comments:

> Forty-four years ago when I was a ceramics student, I couldn't possibly have anticipated how enduring and compelling my sense of playfulness would continue to be to my work process. Yet, to the one studio assistant who works alongside me each year, I'm still communicating this message in various ways: 'If you come through your apprenticeship here knowing how to play, you'll have absorbed the most important lesson I have to teach you.' What first attracted me to pottery was con-

Wall panel, Mantel Series, *with fruit, letter, ewer and leaf by John Glick, 1996–7. Stoneware and porcelain with slips, glazes and oxide washes; multiple firings to cone 10 reduction, salt/soda. 28 x 33 x 11cm. Extruded, constructed.*

PHOTOGRAPH BY JOHN GLICK. © THE ARTIST

necting to people through my hands, placing me in a long-standing craft tradition. The responses of people who experience special satisfaction in using my work and who sense the joy in its creation gratify me deeply. This intrinsic connection – maker to user – feels especially needed in our complicated world.

55

ROBERTA LAIDMAN

Roberta Laidman was first introduced to the technique of slab-building by the Dutch sculptor Marijke van Vlaardingen, in the late 1970s. In 1987 she had an opportunity to work with the Belgian figurative sculptor José Vermeersch, who suggested that she make ceramic dog sculptures. Roberta comments: 'I jumped at this suggestion. I was then, and still am, intensely enamoured of dogs. I relate to them on an intuitive level and admire them for their integrity. Dogs have become my primary metaphor.'

Roberta built upon the knowledge of slab-building that she acquired from Marijke van Vlaardingen, José Vermeersch, and another Dutch sculptor, Frans Duckers, and cites all three as having 'a profound influence' on her work. She went on to produce a book in which she described her slab-building technique in detail for other 'slab sculptors', both beginners and experienced artists wanting to work on a larger scale.

At her studio in Missouri, USA, Roberta continues to slab-build unique ceramic dog

OPPOSITE: **Beverly** *by Roberta Laidman (USA). Stoneware with oxides, engobes and transparent glaze, 52 x 32 x 56cm.* PHOTOGRAPH BY SCOTT McCUE. © THE ARTIST

sculptures. Prior to starting work on a sculpture, she makes several preparatory drawings to gain a better understanding of the form and an insight into the manner in which the piece is to be constructed. Drawings might be made from actual dogs, photos or created from her imagination. She explains that her 'final objective is not to recreate a realistic representation but rather to convey the elemental nature of "dog"'.

Roberta begins by rolling out several slabs of clay, which are about 13mm (0.5in) thick, using either a rolling pin or a slab roller. The clay used is a medium-grade grogged, light coloured, stoneware body that has a firing range of cone 6 to cone 10. Roberta prefers using sculpture clay bodies that have this firing range for their workability, but chooses to glaze fire at lower temperatures: 'Since I'm not making ceramic casserole dishes, I really don't need to go to a higher temperature.'

Roberta Laidman pushes the clay from inside the form, whilst a wooden paddle is used as support on the outside.

Various objects are used to support the form during construction.

PHOTOGRAPHS BY MARK PALMER

Elsa *by Roberta Laidman. Stoneware with oxides, engobes and transparent glaze, 43 x 33 x 50cm.*

PHOTOGRAPH BY SCOTT McCUE. © THE ARTIST

The slabs are laid out on a canvas surface and allowed to dry sufficiently until they are ready to work with, that is when a slab will stand without support when balanced on its edge. They are then stacked eight or ten high, separated by sheets of plastic, and wrapped tightly in more plastic until required.

The first step in the creation of a sculpture is to place a 'cornerstone' slab in position. Roberta then proceeds, gradually adding further slabs as the form is firm enough to take them. She works from the inside out, and avoids touching the outside surface of the clay as much as possible, in an effort to retain 'the natural flesh-like quality that the slabs have when they are first rolled out on canvas'. She presses on the slabs from the inside with her fingers or a small rubber rib, whilst simultaneously countering the pressure on the outside, using a wooden paddle or the heel of her hand.

By working on several sculptures at once, Roberta can allow one piece to dry sufficiently for work to continue on it, while proceeding with other forms. She stresses the importance of not attempting to carry on working on a piece when the clay is too soft to support itself as successive slabs are joined, and also cautions against overworking any one area of clay.

Tubes made from slabs are used to form various sections, such as legs, muzzles, torsos for standing dogs, and necks. Some of these separate parts are made in advance, as Roberta explains: 'I keep several picnic coolers filled with pre-rolled slabs and clay "body parts". Some parts are made especially for the current work, while others are recycled from earlier pieces that didn't work.'

Two basic dressmaking techniques are used in shaping specific areas: a section of slab can be expanded by inserting a gusset – a wedge-shaped piece of clay; or reduced by making a dart – removing a triangular-shaped area of clay. These techniques are used respectively for flaring out or narrowing in sections of a sculpture.

Various means are used to support the structure on the outside as work continues. Roberta refers to these as 'external armatures', and uses items such as whole bricks and brick parts to prop up the sculptures at various stages.

Other methods used include soft insulation kiln building bricks carved to the exact shape required to support a particular form, and a sling made from a strip of fabric suspended from a wooden frame.

When the sculpture is still at the leatherhard stage, a clear glaze is applied to the eyes and any other areas that Roberta wants 'to preserve in a pristine state'. The finished forms are placed in an electric kiln while leatherhard to complete the drying process. The work is then preheated at a very low temperature for between 8 and 10 hours, before biscuit firing to cone 04. Roberta explains that the main advantage of this preheat is that it avoids having to move the sculptures while they are at the fragile, bone dry stage. Another advantage is that it reduces the overall period of time from construction to the final glaze firing.

Just as the sculptures require external armatures when they are being constructed, they also require support during both the biscuit and glaze firings. Roberta uses various pieces of kiln furniture, stilts and soft insulation bricks to prop up those parts of sculptures that may slump during firing such as cantilevered heads, or bodies standing on fragile legs.

After biscuit firing, a wash of fifty per cent iron and fifty per cent manganese is applied. The oxides seep into the surface cavities accentuating the texture. Excess oxide is wiped off using a damp cloth or sponge. Engobes mixed with body stains provide the basic colour palette and are applied by brushing, sponging or spraying. Work on details of eyes, tongue and nails is completed and a clear glaze is sprayed on sparingly. The sculpture is then glazed fired to cone 02 in an electric kiln.

In discussing her use of the slab-building technique, Roberta states that: 'Respect for the structural nature of the clay is key to the slab-building technique. Patience is essential. The clay shouldn't be over-handled, or the process rushed.'

JIM ROBISON

Jim Robison creates a wide variety of ceramics including large-scale sculptures commissioned for installation in public buildings and outdoor areas; sculptural garden furniture; large vessel forms and on a more domestic scale – dishes and planters, all from slabs of clay. Originally from Missouri, USA, Jim has long been a resident of Yorkshire in the north of England, and it is the landscape and geographical features of this area that are the primary inspiration for his work.

Jim explains that he was initially drawn to working in clay since:

Ceramics seemed to offer the widest potential for creative thought and expression. Each surface could be an exploration of painting, printmaking; a recording of brushwork, mark

Tatton Park Festival Sculpture *by Jim Robison (USA/UK). Stoneware, height 2.5m.*
PHOTOGRAPH BY IAN MARSH. © THE ARTIST

making and impressions. The material could be thrown, modelled or constructed. Forms could be functional, sculptural or indeed, architectural. Colour and texture possibilities are vast. And best of all, firings could render these things permanent. Durable, colour fast, suitable for functional items, but also for sculptures, murals and outdoor installations.

The first stage in the production of each piece in Jim's repertoire involves rolling out slabs of clay, often using a roller which he made by adapting a mangle, originally used during the Victorian era for wringing water out of clothes after washing. Slabs of up to 45cm (18in) in

Slip decorated slabs are passed through the slab roller again to stretch and distort the combed and incised patterns.

PHOTOGRAPH BY JIM ROBISON AND IAN MARSH

width can be accommodated on this slab roller, and Jim explains that when he first began using it:

> [The roller] set off a train of thought that required the sheets or slabs of clay to be rolled over and over again. Roller pressures created unusual edges and stretched patterns. Multiple layers of clay resulted in stressed surfaces and torn openings. So instead of making quick and uniform slabs, repeat rolling became part of a longer process where edges, openings and markings were planned, developed, tried and tested. Lengthy manipulations were undertaken in an effort to create surfaces that appear to have a history; geological formations in the making.

Jim now also uses a commercial slab roller with a 75cm (30in) wide bed, so that larger slabs can be made and manipulated. Slabs are made in advance before starting work on a particular piece, and left to stiffen on several layers of newspaper. When working on large-scale pieces, slabs are stacked up with newspaper in between, and are then wrapped in polythene until required. Several different clays are used, all of which have a high grog content. Those with the coarsest grog are used for the largest sculptural work, while the smoother bodies are used both in making smaller pieces and also in creating extruded details for the larger work. Whether using the homemade or commercial slab roller, the cloth on which the slabs are rolled out 'transfers an immediate richness to the clay surface'.

While the slabs are still flat, they are decorated with a white slip, made up from a porcelain body, and coloured slips, made by adding stains and oxides to the porcelain slip. Several

61

Curved wooden formers are used to shape and support large slabs of clay. Wooden laths are attached to the back of the slabs to prevent warping during drying.

PHOTOGRAPH BY JIM ROBISON AND IAN MARSH

different methods are used to create a variety of surface effects and textures. Slips are brushed, stencilled, combed and trailed over textures and cloth stencils. In some instances, narrow strips of clay are attached to a large slab and combed, before the slab is passed through the roller again. In this way the combed patterns are stretched and distorted.

In making a large outdoor vase for example, the slip-decorated and textured slabs are placed in curved plywood formers, the largest of which are approximately 1m (39in) in height.

The slabs are allowed to stiffen to soft leather-hard before the formers are raised into a vertical position, and the slabs joined to a base slab. In some instances, wooden dowels or laths are temporarily attached to the back of the slabs before they are stood upright to provide support and prevent warping as the form continues to dry. The two parts of the form are then joined at the edges, and the joins strengthened with coils of clay. Additional processes may be carried out on the surfaces at this stage, slips applied or smaller slabs of textured clay with torn edges attached.

In addition to slab rollers, Jim also uses extruders to create components for his work. He explains: 'Extruders have expanded the range of my making possibilities. Discovery of them was like a breath of fresh air in the

Large Vase Form *by Jim Robison. Stoneware, with porcelain slips. Height 1m.*

PHOTOGRAPH BY JIM ROBISON. © THE ARTIST

studio.' When he first began using an extruder, 'extrusions became a focus of considerable work with the trials and errors involved providing exciting impetus to the work. Extruders do require a bit of mechanical inclination, especially if you wish to develop dies and profiles to stamp your own identity on things.'

Jim uses the extruder in many different ways: to make coils for use in handbuilding; hollow tubes to be used as structural supports in the construction of large sculptures and murals; extruded sections for rims, feet, handles and other details that 'give a precision finish to these aspects of the piece'. Extruded sections are often used to frame slabs, both in large-scale works and also small functional pieces.

Jim makes work that is much taller than the maximum height of his kiln, 120cm (47in), by constructing separate modules that are joined after firing. Most pieces are raw glazed and single fired. Ash-based glazes are sprayed on in several thin layers to achieve a dry fired surface finish, with subtle variations in tone. A range of other glazes is also used in specific areas to create contrasts in colour and surface. The translucent nature of thin glaze layers allows the colours of slips and clay to show through. The work is fired to 1280°C in reduction, in a 1.4cu m (50cu ft) gas-fired kiln, with firings taking 24 hours, including an overnight preheat.

Discovering solutions to technical problems is a process that Jim enjoys, and making and decorating techniques provide the inspiration for further exploration. The textures and colour variations of the surfaces achieved using these processes reflect his surroundings, both natural and manmade.

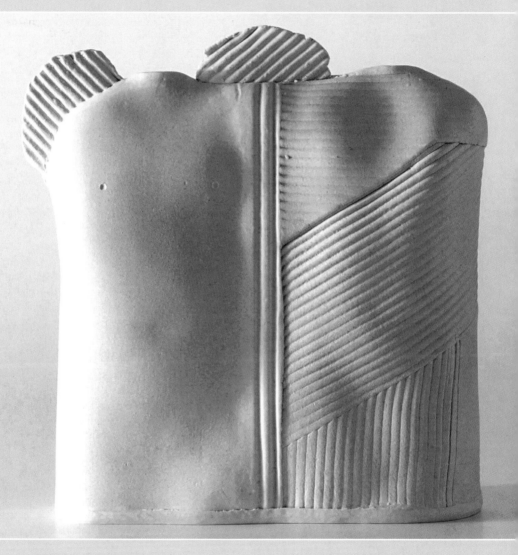

In the 1990s, Vladimir Tsivin's work concentrated on slab-built torso forms, inspired by the figurative sculptures of ancient and classical civilizations. In these evocative sculptures, gentle undulations in the surface textures, which are suggestive of clothing, subtly hint at human forms beneath.

Eros and Bride *by Vladimir Tsivin (Russia), 1990. Stoneware, height 27.5cm.*

PHOTOGRAPH BY MICHAEL HARVEY.
COURTESY OF GALERIE BESSON. © THE ARTIST

Trois Maisons *by Camille Virot (France), 2004. Slabs joined by glaze during firing; base made from refractory cement. The glaze was covered in lime before firing.* © THE ARTIST

Leaves II *by Terry O'Farrell (Ireland), 2006. An installation of six leaf forms, each 30cm long. Low fired porcelain.*

PHOTOGRAPH BY JOHN CROWLEY. © THE ARTIST

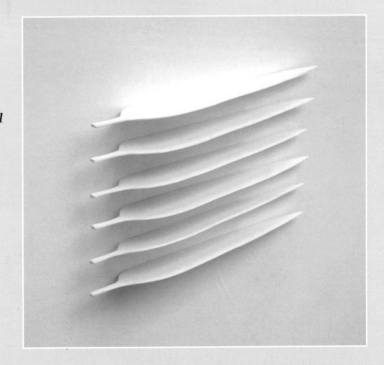

The slabs for the leaf forms in **Leaves II** were rolled paper-thin by hand. Steel needle rods support the work when mounting, with the pieces placed just below eye level making them almost invisible at first glance.

65

‘ Part of the reason for making (in fact a very large part of the reason) is to see things that I have never seen before – to build something that I cannot fully understand or explain. I do not make functional pots, but rather use the vessel as a subject to give form and meaning to an expression. The content of a vessel is literally the space within it – a vessel defines an emptiness as a presence. Working with ceramics, I can be both builder and painter: can handle shape and structure, as well as exploring

Field *by Ken Eastman (UK), 2002. Height 55cm. White stoneware, painted with layers of slips and oxides and fired several times to 1180°C.* PHOTOGRAPH BY KEN EASTMAN. © THE ARTIST

tone and colour. I do not directly plan or draw the piece of work before it is made: ideas that work in two dimensions are often different from those that are successful in three dimensions. Drawing enables me to approach the spirit that I want the work to have. ’

ABOVE: Form by Torbjørn Kvasbø, 2003.
55 x 80 x 140cm. Made at the European
Ceramic Work Centre (EKWC),
the Netherlands. In the collection
of the Sørlandets Kunstmuseum,
Kristiansand, Norway.

PHOTOGRAPH: ALF GEORG DANNEVIG. © THE ARTIST

LEFT: Torbjørn Kvasbø (Norway) working
on a large slab-built sculpture in La Borne,
France. PHOTOGRAPH BY PHILIPPE LANGLOIS

Standing Form *by*
Coll Minogue. Stoneware,
wood-fired, height 22cm.
Collection of James Kasper
and Lucy Hansen, USA.
PHOTOGRAPH BY DAVID VAN ALLEN.
© THE ARTIST

' One of the aspects of working with clay that
most interests me is the material's ability to
accept and retain marks and impressions.
Within the range of possible woodfire effects,
it is the quieter, paler ones that appeal most
to me, such as those to be found on early
German stonewares, and also on some of the
traditional stoneware produced in La Borne
in central France. Marks made in the clay
surface are subtly accentuated by this quiet
range of colours. '

Cradle, slipware, Staffordshire, England,
c. 1700. Earthenware, length 40cm.
In the Glaisher Collection of The Fitzwilliam
Museum, Cambridge, England.

© FITZWILLIAM MUSEUM, UNIVERSITY OF CAMBRIDGE (C. 251-1928)

Model of a cooking stove, Chinese, Eastern Han
Dynasty (AD 25–220). Earthenware, with an
iridescent green lead glaze, 7.6 x 23.4cm.

© GLASGOW MUSEUMS: THE BURRELL COLLECTION (38.74)

70

VESSELS

As discussed in the introduction, slab-building has been used as a method of forming functional vessels since as early as 7000 BC. Two further examples of slab-built vessels in a historical context are briefly described in this section.

While many people with an interest in ceramics may be familiar with the unglazed red stoneware Yixing teapots, which have been produced continuously in the Jiangsu province of China since the early Ming dynasty (1368–1644), they may not, however, be aware that these pots are neither thrown nor slipcast, but are in fact slab-built. The local, fine-grained, high iron bearing clays are especially suited to this technique, as they have good strength at the green stage and also a low shrinkage rate (ten per cent).

In addition, the clays have unique properties that make the finished pots particularly suitable for the brewing of tea, retaining the taste, colour and aroma of the leaves, so that tea stays fresher longer. Traditionally these teapots were fired in oxidation to temperatures ranging from 1190° to 1270°C, which meant that the clay was still porous. The methods used to finish the pots resulted in a lightly burnished surface.

Historically the clay was prepared for use by

Teapot, Chinese, Ch'ing Dynasty, nineteenth century. Stoneware, painted in a buff slip with a landscape and bamboo sprays. The loop handle has two loose rings.

beating with large wooden mallets for up to two days until it reached the required consistency for forming the teapots. Today however, except for the most expensive teapots, clay is more likely to be prepared in a pug mill.

Thin slabs of approximately 3mm (0.1in) in thickness are formed from the prepared clay by beating with wooden mallets. In this way, the clay is highly compressed and consequently the slabs are less likely to warp than if they were rolled.

The components from which the pots are formed are then cut very precisely from the slabs, using a range of tools. Once the basic shape has been made, additional forming is carried out by paddling, using light wooden spatulas or paddles.

A vast range of different shapes of Yixing teapots has been produced in the past, and new variations continue in contemporary production. These teapots are generally small in size, often no more than 7.5–10cm (3–4in) or less, in height. The example illustrated opposite, from the National Museum of Scotland in Edinburgh, which dates from the nineteenth century, is 10cm (4in) high to the top of the lid.

In Britain in the seventeenth and eighteenth centuries, included in the well-known slipware pottery produced in Staffordshire, was a range of large dishes that were formed on moulds from flat slabs of earthenware clay. These 'Boar's Head' dishes, such as the one illustrated overleaf, from the Burrell Collection in Glasgow, Scotland, which is more than 50cm (20in) in length, had slip trailed, feathered decoration under a lead glaze.

While the majority of the contemporary

71

'Boar's Head' slipware dish, Staffordshire, England. Earthenware, late seventeenth or eighteenth century. Decorated with stripes of cream and brown-coloured slip, 50.8 x 39.3cm.

© GLASGOW MUSEUMS: THE BURRELL COLLECTION (39.27)

vessels described in this section are ultimately intended for use, for some of the artists, function may not necessarily be their primary concern. Others consider that their work is not complete until it is used in the preparation, cooking or serving of food.

DOUGLASS RANKIN AND WILL RUGGLES

Douglass Rankin and Will Ruggles, who work in North Carolina, USA, make a wide range of ceramics for use, including slab-built vases and dishes for serving food. The slabs from which these pots are made are cut from blocks of clay. Some dishes are made on hump moulds, while others are formed in cloth slings. Amongst the latter are pots that Douglass and Will refer to as either 'funky squares' or 'funky rectangles' depending on their shape, as the finished dishes retain the irregular edges left by their hands while pounding the initial clay block into shape.

It was while both potters were apprentices working with Randy Johnston in the late 1970s, that they learned to cut slabs, as

opposed to rolling them. The technique that they use for making their slab dishes is as follows. Lumps of clay, approximately 11.5kg (25lb) in weight, are spiral wedged and joined carefully, making sure that no air is trapped. The clay is then hand-pounded into a block of the correct shape for the particular dishes being made, and thick enough for the required number of slabs. This is done on a flat work surface. A pair of wooden sticks with notches cut (using a hacksaw), measured and spaced for the required slab thickness, are held vertically with a cutting wire stretched between them. The first set of corresponding notches is a little lower than the top of the clay block. Then carefully keeping tension on the wire while making sure that the sticks remain vertical with their bases flat on the work surface, and starting at

Funky Rectangles *by Douglass Rankin and Will Ruggles (USA). Stoneware, wood-fired to cone 9, salt and soda, 32 x 13 x 5cm.*
PHOTOGRAPH BY WILL RUGGLES. © THE ARTISTS

the far side of the block, the sticks are pulled forward, the wire cutting evenly through the clay. The first cut is to level off the top of the clay block and the uneven top slice is removed. The wire is then lowered by one notch to cut the first slab, and the process continues until the last one has been cut and there is a stack of slabs of the shape and thickness required to make the dishes. The top surface of each slab is slightly compressed using a rib, before it is lifted off carefully so as not to alter the shape and compression, either by exerting excessive pressure or stretching.

Prepared clay and the tools used by Douglass Rankin and Will Ruggles in making slab dishes. Cutting slabs from a shaped block of clay.

Lifting a cut slab from the block of clay.

LEFT: *Compressing the slabs using a rib.*

PHOTOGRAPHS BY
DOUGLASS RANKIN
AND MICHAEL HUNT

Will Ruggles compressing a slab into shape on a cloth support stretched over a wooden frame.

Once removed from the cloth support, the dish is turned over onto a piece of foam placed on top of a former and the back of the slab is compressed to realign the clay particles so that it will hold the new shape. Coils of clay are attached to form feet.

PHOTOGRAPHS BY DOUGLASS RANKIN AND MICHAEL HUNT

The slabs are placed upside-down on a wooden board and the backs are lightly compressed with the rib. Any air bubbles that may be exposed during this process are pierced, pressed in, filled with small balls of clay and integrated by further use of the rib. At this stage, the slab edges are ready to be cut to shape using a template, if necessary for the type of dish being made, or, alternatively, the slabs are left to dry to working consistency.

Different types of slab pots are made whilst the slabs are at various stages of dryness. For slumped slabs that are to have feet attached, Douglass and Will like to work with a slab when it is just sufficiently hard that it almost holds its form when compressed into the required shape. To create the shape, the slab is first pressed into a cloth support stretched over a wooden frame. Next, it is turned over onto a piece of foam placed on top of a suitable form. The back of the slab is compressed to realign the clay particles so that it will hold the new

75

Trimming the ends off the coiled feet.
PHOTOGRAPH BY DOUGLASS RANKIN AND MICHAEL HUNT

shape. Once the feet are attached, the dish is immediately placed the right way up on a ware board while it is still soft enough to allow subtle shape changes to be made, yet firm enough to hold its form.

For dishes formed on bisque hump moulds, Douglass and Will prefer to use clay that is a bit softer so that the slab can be compressed onto the mould without cracking. Will explains that for this process it is best if 'the clay is somewhere in the middle between wet and leatherhard'. He continues:

This method requires good compression evenly applied all over the outside of the slab if we want the pot to 'remember' the new form

through drying and firing. The pot is pulled off the mould as soon as it is dry enough to lift off without much movement. You can use very soft clay on a hump mould, but this requires additional moulds since they absorb more water and the slab releases more slowly. For assembled slab pots like vases, we like to use the clay when it is at a stage similar to that used for hump moulds, about half way to leatherhard. It is just hard enough to hold the shape once it is strengthened by joining the slabs, but not so hard that we can't relatively easily alter the form by squeezing and scraping the clay. If the clay is a bit soft, the scraping can also leave a torn surface that we like.

Since Douglass and Will decorate and glaze at the leatherhard stage, one aspect of slab forming they particularly enjoy is that hump-moulded pots can be decorated while the slabs are still flat. As Douglass puts it:

This method is exciting for several reasons. One is that decorating a flat slab of clay has a totally different 'feeling' than decorating a three-dimensional shape. This opens us to new ideas that a curved shape would not stimulate. Another difference is that the flat form is physically easier to decorate. And finally, we love to see how the decoration changes after shaping it on the hump mould.

The edges of dishes formed on hump moulds are completed as follows. After compressing the slab onto the mould as evenly as possible, so as to minimize warping from uneven compression, the edge is cut at an angle using the mould edge as a guide. The outside edge is then

OPPOSITE: **Oval Dish** *by Douglass Rankin and Will Ruggles. Stoneware, wood-fired to cone 9, salt and soda, 43 x 28 x 10cm. Made on a hump mould.*
PHOTOGRAPH BY WILL RUGGLES. © THE ARTISTS

smoothed and rounded using a soft, damp sponge. Once it has dried sufficiently to become firm on the mould, the dish is removed and allowed to dry further before the inside edge is scraped to the required shape using a fettling knife. The rim is then smoothed using a moist thumb. Finally, the edge of a bamboo tool is rolled across the rim at an angle to make linear indentations one at a time.

Douglass and Will once bought a slab roller, thinking that it would increase their work efficiency. Will continues:

We sold it the next week. The problems for us were that the slabs from the roller were not notably better in terms of evenness of compression; the roller required canvas to roll the slabs, which then got so wet from our soft clay that we would have needed a lot of cloth sheets to roll any quantity of slabs at one time; the slabs had a surface we did not like from the canvas imprint; and the machine's large frame took a lot of room in our small workshop. For us, the cutting method is more efficient in all ways and is not limiting for the slab ware we make. Our largest slabs these days are about 24 x 12 x $^5/_8$in when we cut them, and with our toothy clay body, the forms that we make, and our making methods, we have no problems.

Douglass and Will use a stoneware clay that they make up themselves from a combination of indigenous clays and commercially processed raw materials. The work is raw glazed and decorated with slips and glazes at the leatherhard stage and fired in a three-chamber climbing kiln (noborigama) that they built in 1980.

Clay body, slips and glazes, together with the fired effects resulting from salt, soda and woodash, combine to create the surface qualities that Douglass and Will look for in their work. As with all their pots, the range of slab-built pieces that they make, with their soft forms and warm surfaces, retain the appealing qualities of freshly made pots.

Douglass and Will describe their approach to their work:

Since the spring of 1980, and the first firing of our current wood kiln, we have been captivated by the development and refinement of tools, materials, firing and making methods as vehicles toward lively pots for the home. We have also taken great pleasure in exploring the mysteries of expression within the 'constraints' of pots for daily use. Potters who came before us, those with a sincere interest in making beautiful pots, have passed along their knowledge and inspiration through their work. A pleasing junction of human lip and cup rim, the inner fullness of an eating bowl, the lift of a spout offering tea – we would be crazy not to pay attention to these discoveries. There is nothing final in the development of healthy tradition. In it, each individual, through his or her preferences, carries the exploration of the past forward.

From our making and studying pots, it seems clear that comfort and skill with clay, form, surface and fire can set the groundwork for 'losing one's self' in process. In this absorption, empowered by the search for beauty, the universal values of life force can enter the pots, giving them freedom, vitality and meaning beyond technique. When the pot conveys a feeling of the technical, the expression is limited, but when the pot touches the heart, its expression is limitless.

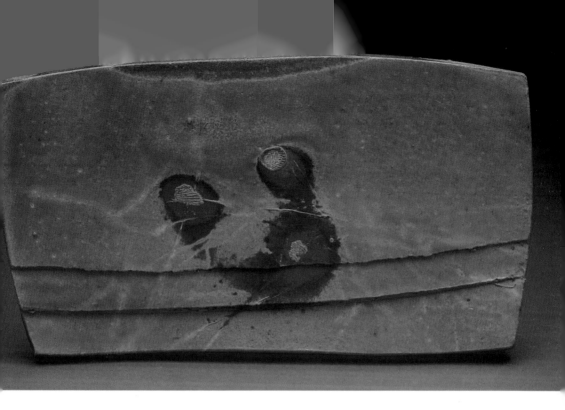

JODY JOHNSTONE

As an apprentice in Bizen, Japan, in the mid 1990s, one of Jody Johnstone's tasks involved using a wooden paddle to make clay slabs for her teacher, Isezaki Jun, to work with. At her studio in Maine, USA, Jody continues this practice of paddling out slabs by hand, making a range of plates and platters, as she explains: 'By hand paddling, I can get the precise thickness that I want throughout the piece. I often paddle my slab a little bit thinner in the middle and thicker around the edges to reduce the weight of the piece without sacrificing its beefy look. As importantly, I like the soft undulations that the paddle leaves on the slab.'

When making her slab plates and platters, Jody prefers to work with clay that 'is a little bit on the hard side'. Once wedged, the clay is pounded into a regularly shaped block by hand. Using the rounded side of a wooden paddle, the block is then beaten flat in a methodical way, and is turned over from time to time as the slab is formed. The paddling process con-

Rectangular Platter by Jody Johnstone (USA). White stoneware, wood-fired for eight days in an anagama. Rice straw and shell marks, 25 x 12cm. PHOTOGRAPH BY DAVID ORSER. © THE ARTIST

tinues until the slab is of the required size and thickness. Jody made the wooden paddles that she uses:

I carved and hand-planed a couple of my own paddles from a four by four piece of lumber while I was still in Japan. I have found that a paddle made from a thick piece of wood, such as a four by four, is much easier to use than the flat type that is widely available commercially, or that is made from a two by four for paddling out slabs. This is because the handle can be high enough to leave room for the fingers to grip it and still be off the table. The handle on my paddle is closer to the flat back than to the face, to allow room for the knuckles. Then the paddling action doesn't make knuckle prints in the slab or, even more importantly, bruise the knuckles on the table.

Jody Johnstone using a wooden paddle to flatten a block of clay to a slab of the required dimensions.

Making a horizontal cut into the slab.

In some recent work, Jody has cut horizontally into the clay slabs from one or more of the edges so as to create variations of depth in the surface of the finished pieces. With the slab lying flat, a cutting wire is held taught and pulled through the clay, close to the surface. Care must be taken not to cut through the thin slice of clay that is created. When the cut has been completed to the required distance towards the centre of the slab, the slice of clay is removed carefully, resulting in a stepped surface with a torn edge. If the clay is too soft at this point, the ripped edge will not be clean enough. The slab is then cut to its final shape using a knife, and is laid on newspaper. Coils of

clay are put in position as supports underneath the paper, to form the slab into the required plate or platter shape. Once the slab has dried sufficiently to hold its shape, Jody thumbs off the knife-cut edges to soften the final look and feel of the piece.

When Jody established her studio, she designed and built an anagama (single chamber tube-shaped woodfire kiln) that was fired for the first time in October 1997. Firings last for a total of eight days. All the work is raw fired. Jody stacks and fires her kiln in much the same way as her teacher in Bizen stacked and fired his kiln. She comments: 'my utilitarian wares lend themselves to a fairly conservative

Tearing away a thin layer of clay from the slab.

Placing coils of clay as supports under the completed slab to form a platter shape.

stacking method, and I end up with a large percentage of pots surviving the firing as firsts.' The paddled plates and platters are generally stacked in the kiln with another pot set on top of them, using either wadding or shells. The placement of the top pot is important, as the flame moving around and under it creates the visual relief or pattern on the plate below. Rice straw is often placed between the pots to achieve decorative fired effects. The shells are not washed before use, and any sand remaining on them is not brushed off especially well. Jody considers that the residual salt in the shells produces 'that beautiful red eye or "flash" around the shell mark'.

In addition to her slab plates and platters, Jody makes a range of thrown tableware and vases. Large garden jars are made by a combination of coiling and throwing. The slab and

Square Platter by Jody Johnstone. Porcelain, wood-fired for eight days in an anagama. Rice straw and shell marks, 18 x 18cm.
PHOTOGRAPH BY DAVID ORSER. © THE ARTIST

wheel-thrown work is made from several commercially blended iron bearing and white stoneware clays. Since a large percentage of her work is unglazed on the outer surfaces, Jody relies on the clay body and placement of the pieces in the kiln to achieve a wide range of wood-fired effects.

Jody says of her work: 'In my pots, I strive for strong and direct forms that embody my sense of beauty and rightness. The anagama firing is integral to the look of my pots. At this point I couldn't give up the richness and depth of my long firings.'

PETRA REYNOLDS

While many ceramists who concentrate on making vessels for use may include some slab-built work in their repertoire, not very many use slab-building techniques in making their entire range. Petra Reynolds, who works in Herefordshire, England, produces a wide variety of slab forms, including jugs, oval dishes, beakers, vases, colanders, teapots and butter dishes. She has developed a method of working that involves using 'patterns' made from card as templates for cutting out variously shaped slabs of clay, that are mitred, bent and joined to create the desired forms.

The method used to construct a butter dish is representative of the techniques Petra uses in making her range of work.

To begin, clay is rolled out to the required thickness using a slab roller. Card templates, one for the lid of the dish and the second for the base, are placed on the slab and the shapes are cut out. Once the shaped slab for the lid section has dried to the correct consistency, the edges to be joined are mitred before being scored and slip applied. They are then pressed together, and a piece of thin canvas is placed over the joins and rubbed from the back so that they are compressed and softened but still quiet evident, creating a strong visual feature in the finished form. Alternatively, a small roller is sometimes used to compress joins. Next, a shape is cut from a thinner hand-rolled slab of clay to form the looped handle for the butter dish lid. This slab is folded around to form a tube, before a tri-angular-shaped section is cut from it, thus allowing it to be bent into shape. The loop is then attached to the lid. The edges of the slab, which will form the base of the dish, are beaten with a wooden baton to achieve a thicker rim. As with the top, the edges to be joined are mitred, scored and slip is applied before they are pressed together to make the base shape. The base is then covered in slip and finger wiped to create a soft striped pattern.

All Petra's work is made from a stoneware

Petra Reynolds using a cardboard template to cut the shape for a butter dish lid from a clay slab.

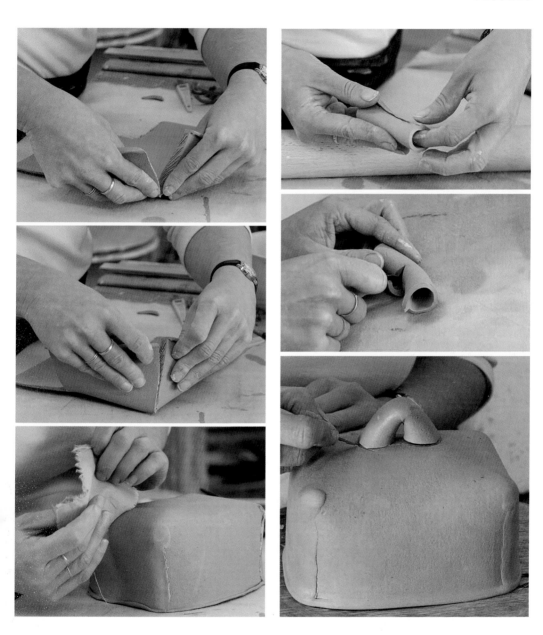

Having been mitred, scored and slipped, the edges of the butter dish lid are brought together and joined. A piece of canvas is then used to compress and soften the join.

A small hollow tube made from a thin slab of clay is cut in the centre, and then bent to form the handle for the butter dish lid.

PHOTOGRAPHS BY J. P. KAVANAGH

A pattern is transferred to the butter dish lid by making marks on the back of a slip-coated paper towel, placed on the clay surface.
PHOTOGRAPH BY J. P. KAVANAGH

clay body, which is a blend of English ball clays and china clay, with the addition of four per cent nepheline syenite. It is once fired to 1300°C in a 0.76m³ (27ft³) 'Olsen-type' fast-fire, woodfire kiln, and soda-glazed 'to provide a spontaneous and varied glazed surface'. Pots are raw glazed on the inside when leatherhard.

Coloured slips of various consistencies are layered onto the exterior of pots at the leather-hard stage by pouring or brushing, with paper resist also sometimes used to achieve contrasting areas of colour. To further decorate the surfaces of her work, Petra uses a form of print-making with slips, often creating linear compositions. One side of a paper hand towel is coated with black slip, and allowed to stiffen to leatherhard. It is then placed slip side down on the surface of a pot. Petra uses various tools, her knuckles or finger tips to apply pressure to the back of the towel, thus imprinting marks in slip, from the paper onto the clay surface.

Petra explains that the inspiration for the decoration of her work comes from many different sources:

I have great admiration for the subtle simplicity and seductive pattern-making found in so much folk art. Japanese 'Oribe' and the African Kuba fabrics, for example. The ever-changing beautiful landscape of Hereford-shire where I live and work is a constant source for ideas. As well as other rural landscapes, there is the contrasting terraced, urban environment of the south-east, an affection that stems back to my family roots. Sketching, simplifying and abstracting these different elements bring a new vocabulary of

Teapot *by Petra Reynolds (UK). Stoneware, applied slip, wood-fired, soda-glazed, height 20cm.* © THE ARTIST

marks and composition to life. Motifs are drawn from an array of different objects. Many of these derive from the tools of everyday rituals such as cooking and gardening, which are so closely linked with my making. Others are found closer to nature, often where time and erosion by the elements have distorted and softened their original form: old buildings, rusty nails, seed pods ... From playful experimentation with line and composition, sketches evolve further on paper into monochrome or colour mono print and collagraph. This has recently become a more important development in the realization of ideas.

Butter Dish *by Petra Reynolds.*
Stoneware, applied slip, wood-fired,
soda-glazed, 10 x 18cm. © THE ARTIST

The effects created by the combination of woodfiring and soda glazing are an important element in Petra's work. The edges of linear patterns 'drawn' in slip, and of dots and other areas of slip applied to the surfaces of pots, are softened by the action of the woodash and the soda so as to blend in easily with the surrounding background area. The firing process is also very much in harmony with the softly rounded forms of Petra's slab-built pots.

RANDY JOHNSTON AND JAN MCKEACHIE JOHNSTON

Randy Johnston and Jan McKeachie Johnston share a studio in Wisconsin, USA. Both artists are interested in the sculptural aspects of functional forms and include many slab-built pieces in the range of vessel forms that they make.

Randy and Jan use a similar technique in initially forming slabs, which is a method that Randy first gained experience of when he spent a period of some seven months working and studying with Tatsuzo Shimaoka in Mashiko, Japan, in 1975. At that time, there were twelve people working in Shimaoka's studio, two of whom were press moulders, as Randy explains:

> Observing their techniques was my first extensive exposure to using flat pieces of clay to generate volumetric forms by pressing them into plaster moulds. These slabs were cut from a large block of wedged clay using sticks held vertically on each side of the block. There were slots cut into each stick and a wire stretched taut between. The cut slots determined the thickness of the slab. When I returned from Japan, I included the making of square trays, covered boxes and vases in my work.

Having used this technique for some time, Randy decided to dispense with the plaster moulds:

> A quick boredom with plaster moulds led through evolution of technique to the use of plywood slump forms and basic paper patterns derived from geometric shapes. This is a similar technique to sheet metal and silversmith working. It is known as the process of planes to solids.
>
> This technique provided a more active tactile and visual engagement, especially with the clay surface of the exterior of the form and

A plywood (cutout) former used for supporting slabs of clay when making lids and boat forms. Positive and negative shaped formers used for supporting small boat forms. A small boat form supported on a curved wooden former.

> a freedom from form and surface predetermined by a plaster mould. Paper patterns can be derived from a drawing or from an assembled and deconstructed form.

In addition to shapes cut from slabs of clay, Randy sometimes uses extruded components to form parts such as 'the lips of vases, box inset flanges and skirts or feet for vases' in creating his slab-built forms. He first determines the shape that is required by modelling a coil of clay, and then cuts an extruder die based on the cross-section of the piece.

When Randy is making one of his 'boat forms', the initial shaping is done by draping a slab of clay into a plywood cutout support. Sometimes a slab of clay that has been impressed with a rope pattern is used for making these forms, with the patterned surface on the interior. The slab slumps into the opening in the plywood, thus creating the basic shape for the form, which is often further defined by hand. Excess clay is trimmed, and the slab is

Randy Johnston adding final details to a small boat form.

PHOTOGRAPH BY LOIS WILKINS

OPPOSITE: **Boat Form** *by Randy Johnston (USA). Wood-fired stoneware, length 70cm. Initial shaping was done in a curved plywood form.*

PHOTOGRAPH BY PETER LEE. © THE ARTIST

allowed to stiffen to leatherhard supported in the plywood shape. Once it is firm enough to be handled without distorting, it is removed and placed between 'positive and negative' shaped wood forms, where it takes on a gently curved shape. It is then left to dry in an upside-down position. Later, a rim, made from either a hand-formed coil or an extruded shape, is attached to the slab and final details are added. Randy comments that his love of boats and hull forms is the inspiration for these pieces.

While much of Jan's work is thrown and altered, she also makes some slab-built pieces, including a range of vase forms. One particular type of vase has flat sides and is sometimes made from textured slabs of clay. A brayer – a rolling tool used by printmakers – is used to create texture by rolling first in one direction in parallel lines on the surface of a soft slab, and then rolling at right angles to the first series of lines, thus creating a soft crosshatch-type pattern. The sides of the vase are cut from slabs using paper templates. When the components for the vase have stiffened to a suitable condition for working, a long narrow slab is joined to the inside edge of one of the flat side slabs, the second slab is then placed in position on top, and also joined. Later the form is tidied up and any finishing details added. This type of vase is sometimes made with two separate compartments for flowers.

Randy and Jan biscuit fire all their work for ease of handling when applying slip and glazes. A range of semi-vitreous flashing slips is applied after biscuit firing. Some pieces, glazed with a dry Shino-type glaze, are then gas-fired. This glaze breaks on the edges of forms, adding further 'textural nuances'. However,

Jan McKeachie Johnston using a printmaking roller to create an impressed pattern on slabs.

Constructing a vase from slabs that were cut using a paper template.

PHOTOGRAPHS BY LOIS WILKINS

Jan McKeachie Johnston completing a slab-built vase.

PHOTOGRAPH BY LOIS WILKINS

Double Envelope Vase *by Jan McKeachie Johnston (USA). Slab construction with two flower-containing areas. Wood-fired stoneware.* PHOTOGRAPH BY PETER LEE. © THE ARTIST

most work is wood-fired, either for three days in a large two-chamber climbing kiln (noborigama) or for five days in a single-chamber tube kiln (anagama). Randy comments: 'Through the extended woodfiring process, ash is deposited on the surface of the work in ways that enhance the surface textures and accentuate planes and details of the pieces. Each kiln and firing method allows us to explore a range of flame shapes and oxidation and reduction conditions, resulting in a range of colour and texture choices.'

Jan describes her approach to her work:

> While much of my work, such as plates, bowls and cups, is made on the wheel, other forms are created using a combination of throwing and

handbuilding techniques, and some from slabs exclusively. When using slabs, I often use paper patterns as templates, much like sewing. The parts are cut and then curved or folded to fit them together before joining the 'seams'.

> The slab work has been inspired by excitement about certain forms and sensibilities of surface that were not possible to achieve from a thrown piece of clay.

Of his work, Randy says:

> There are constant references in my work to sculptors, painters and cultures whose work appeals to me both in an intellectual and visceral sense. Works of primitive cultures are the most intriguing. Examples would be

Stacking Box *by Randy Johnston. Wood-fired stoneware, 33 x 28 x 12.5cm. Slab-built using paper patterns for lid and side walls. The inner lips between the stacked layers were extruded. White slip was applied at the biscuit stage, and black areas printed using a cut sponge. This piece was 'influenced by Japanese stacking boxes used for food at celebrations'.*

PHOTOGRAPH BY PETER LEE.
© THE ARTIST

the Cycladic and African cultures. In my work there is a layering process that I am intrigued with.

This layering brings me to a sacred place, a memory of a perfect place where we can stop and play with our voices, with the sounds we can make. Constructing, layering, listening to the echoes. This space also exists often within the architectural structures of our work as we attempt to define space, design structure and deal with symbolic interpretations. The complex of social interaction and place of our humanity within this structure is in large part a continuing expression of my conversation with the material and process of clay.

GAIL NICHOLS

At her studio in rural New South Wales, some 300km south-west of Sydney, Australia, Gail Nichols specializes in making soda-glazed vessels, many of them large in scale, in which function is not necessarily a primary concern. All of these forms, including a range of 'Wave Plates' begin on the wheel. Gail explains that she often uses slab techniques in conjunction with her thrown work: 'I prefer not to make rigid distinctions between throwing and hand-building; they are all part of the clay-working process. I regularly move pieces on and off the wheel, forming and manipulating them with whatever technique is most appropriate at the time. I enjoy exploiting the plastic properties of clay.'

To make a wave plate, Gail begins by throwing a large disc that is thinner at the centre, then increases in thickness and tapers to a thin outer edge. When completed, a wire cut is made between the disc and bat it was thrown on. A thick piece of foam rubber is then placed on top, and the bat, disc and foam are turned over. Another cut with the wire releases the disc from the bat, which is then removed, leaving the soft clay disc lying on the foam. The cut surface is smoothed with a rubber kidney. Then, using a block of wood, three deep impressions are made into the thicker section of the clay, simultaneously forming indentations in the centre of the disc, as well as three feet on which the completed wave plate will stand. When pieces of foam rubber are placed underneath to lift and support the sides of the plate, the rim naturally assumes an undulating wave pattern. The wave plate is then allowed to stiffen in this position on the foam. When it is sufficiently firm, it is lifted onto a wooden bat and allowed to dry.

Gail comments on the wave plates made in this way:

Gail Nichols throwing a disc.

A thrown slab has the advantage that the thickness can be deliberately varied to suit the form and subsequent manipulations. With my wave plates, I enjoy the fact that there is a subtle wave in the clay's cross-section, induced by the throwing process, as well as in the more obvious undulations of the plate form itself. The thicker part of the cross-section has a practical application as well; it is nicely placed to allow deep impressions to be made, forming the three feet.

For many years, Gail has been carrying out research into the effects that are achievable in soda glazing (receiving a PhD in the subject in 2002). The vessels that she makes, including large, voluminous thrown and altered jar forms with gently undulating surfaces, bowls in a range of sizes, and the wave plates, are made with the soda-glaze process in mind. All work is made from a high alumina, white stoneware body that is lightly grogged, and is once-fired to Orton cone 10/11, in a gas-fired kiln.

Gail Nichols turning the thrown disc, which is still attached to the throwing bat, over onto a piece of foam rubber.

TOP: *A block of wood is used to create three deep impressions in the disc.*

ABOVE: *Pieces of foam are used to prop up and support the rim of the disc, forming a wave plate.*

No glazes or slips are applied to the surface of the work prior to firing. All the surface colours and textures are achieved as a result of the introduction of soda (sodium carbonate) and variation in atmosphere in the kiln during firing. The interaction of the clay body and soda vapour results in a harmonious integration of surface and form. While some of the thrown forms may alter shape during firing, the wave plates only alter slightly, and Gail comments that they are far more stable in the firing than they might appear. She adds that the highly crystalline, soda-glaze surface created during the firing does appear to soften the form of these plates.

Regarding the firing of the wave plates Gail observes:

The form of the wave plate is particularly suited to my process of soda vapour glazing, in which I aim for the firing dynamics to be evident in the finished work. A wave plate has the capacity to 'play' with the flame, directing vapour over, under and around the clay form,

Two completed wave plates drying.

PHOTOGRAPHS BY DAVE NELSON

creating exposed areas of glaze and shadowed areas of flashing that complement the form's curves and indentations.

Gail places all her work in the kiln on wads, with the type of wadding used varying according to the form, where it fits in the pack, and what sort of marks she wants to create on the work. Seashells are often used, with the wave plates usually placed on oyster shells, which are set onto wads made from kaolin and sand. The placement of wads affects atmospheric flashing on the surface of the forms, creating areas of warm red and orange tones. Other surface colours achieved on the work include subtle shades of green, grey, brown and, on some pieces, blue. The dominant surface effect, however, is often what Gail refers to as a 'white, icy, dimpled matt glaze'.

When asked about the development of the wave plate form, Gail gave the following account:

The wave plates have often been compared to stingrays. I admit there is a similarity in form there, but it is coincidental, not intentional. The origin of the plates actually occurred on a much more abstract level, based on ideas of rhythm and movement. I make a practice of allowing myself 'free-play' time in the studio, when I simply play with clay, manipulating it in various ways. I do this without any aim of actually producing a finished piece. It is essentially a process of three-dimensional sketching, and often the movement of the manipulated clay is enough to suggest some new ideas.

The wave plates evolved from a series of such experiments. I was fascinated by the way a slab of clay would move and hold its new shape if pushed with a block of wood into a pad of foam rubber. Negative spaces on one side would become positive spaces on the other. The simplicity of the process intrigued me, as well as the natural rhythms created in the form, making the clay seem to come to life.

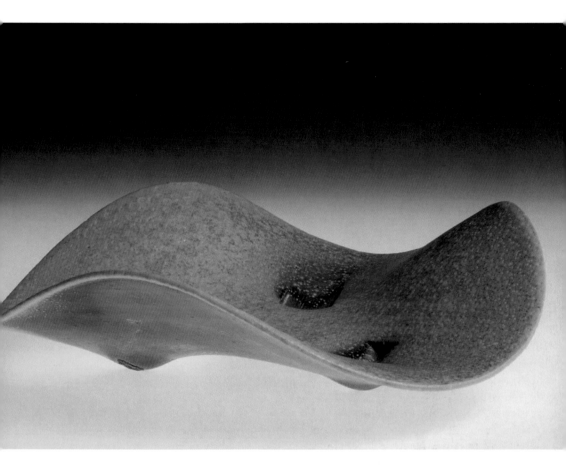

This form also showed wonderful potential for playing with flame and vapour movement in the kiln. Initially, I worked with small rectangular slabs and four indentations/feet. As I moved into larger scale, I found a thrown slab was useful in that I could easily vary the thickness according to where the indentations were to be made later, so the slabs became circular. I found that three indentations/feet made a more stable form, and encouraged a nice wave movement around the circumference. All this made for a very satisfying blend of ideal and practical design.

Gail continues to explore the wave plate concept in her slab work, developing an even

Wave Plate *by Gail Nichols (USA/Australia).*
Stoneware, soda-glazed, diameter 40cm.
PHOTOGRAPH BY MICHEL BROUET. © THE ARTIST

higher alumina clay body and a new series of robust pieces featuring a generosity of material and landscaped textured surfaces, as she explains:

Like much of my work, this new range evolved from an exercise in problem-solving with materials and process. I had developed a very high alumina clay body which vitrifies well at Orton cone 10. The body has very low plasticity and would be deemed by many to be

95

unworkable, a bit like modelling kiln wash. I persevered with it because I was fascinated by the colour and textural response when soda fired, and the potential to work with more weighty sculptural forms. Throwing is not really an option with this clay. Slabs are made by repeatedly dropping a piece of clay onto a flat, absorbent surface, picking it up, turning a bit, and dropping again. The thick slab is then cut with a coiled piece of wire, set on a piece of foam rubber, and manipulated from above and below. The foam rubber

Wave Pair *by Gail Nichols, 2006. Stoneware, soda-glazed, each 5 x 11 x 11cm.*

PHOTOGRAPH BY MICHEL BROUET. © THE ARTIST

supports the form and also prevents finger marks and other unwanted indentations in the clay surface.

The aim is to create rhythmic movement and distortions in the form while retaining the freshness of the wire cut, as if the piece grew of its own accord.

GALLERY

Vase *by* Linda Christianson (USA), 1990. Stoneware, wood-fired, salt-glazed, 30 x 7.5 x 30cm.
© THE ARTIST

‘ In making the vases, the two methods I employ utilize either a slab made on the table by hand or cutting up a thrown form and laying the form down flat onto the table. Drawings are made on paper, and a silhouette is selected and cut out. After initially forming either the handmade or thrown slab, I pay a lot of attention to the surface of the clay. I think of it as fabric, and try to impart a repetitive but irregular pattern using my hand, or a tool of some sort. A rim can be incorporated into the slab at this point. Laying the silhouette on the slab, I cut out the shape. Next, the silhouette is flipped over, and a second shape cut out. A rough bottom for the vase is cut out and placed on a bat. Assemblage is accomplished by mitring the corners, much in the way one would construct the form out of wood, and scoring and slipping all of the parts, I pay particular attention to the seams. On the inside of the form coils are added on all seams, compressing them well. The exterior seams are pressed together just enough to seal them without obliterating the surface of the material. It takes a delicate but firm touch, much like handling a kitten or a baby. The exterior of the base is seamed by pushing the base up into the pot, much like working with pie dough. The form is put on the wheel, and the base/wall seam trimmed with a wooden stick. It is then smoothed with a rib and undercut. A form needing a foot would be flipped over after initial setting up, and a coil, or sled runner shaped foot attached. ’

ABOVE: Chest *by Jan-Åke Andersson (Sweden). Stoneware, leaf impressions, wood-fired in an anagama, four day firing to a maximum temperature of 1325°C. 15 x 26 x 14cm.*

© THE ARTIST

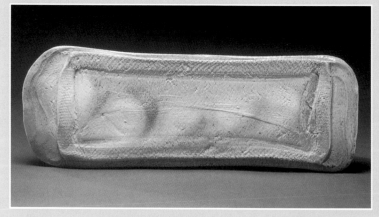

Stretched Slab Tray *by Robert Sanderson (UK). Porcelain with added Molochite, wood-fired. Length 40cm. Collection of James Kasper and Lucy Hansen, USA.*

PHOTOGRAPH BY DAVID VAN ALLEN. © THE ARTIST

Furrowed Platter *by Catherine White (USA).*
Stoneware, natural ash glaze, anagama
wood-fired, 5 x 45 x 23cm.
PHOTOGRAPH BY WARREN FREDERICK. © THE ARTIST

' Stoneware clay is pounded and rolled out into
a slab almost 2.5cm (1in) thick. A large loop
trimming tool is used to cut the furrows. The
edges are propped up with wooden dowels as
the slab dries, topside up. The platter was fired
on edge, leaning against the wall of an anagama kiln during a three day firing. The kiln's
temperature range is from Orton cone 13
(front) to cone 7 (rear); this platter was about
cone 10. '

Continental Plate *by Simon Reece
(Australia), from Iced Earth Series.
Stoneware, woodash and rice hull ash
glaze, 10 x 26 x 25cm. Fired in a gas
kiln, 30 hour firing.*

❛ The clay for these compressed slabs is a mixture of a sandy fireclay and a porcelain clay. The clay mass for the continental plates, generally 9kg, is torn, sgraffitoed with fingers and any other tool available, impressed with rocks or bricks and then compressed down, with me sitting or jumping on a plaster platter mould, to form a slab. The slab is then carved out underneath to lighten the mass and liberate the piece for utilitarian use.

The tearing and compressing place immense stresses on the clay, and the sandy fireclay seems to be essential to counteract the clay memory and hence cracking. Even so, I am continually patching cracks during the drying process. This technique has evolved from that taught to me by my teacher, Uneo San, in Bizen, Japan. ❜

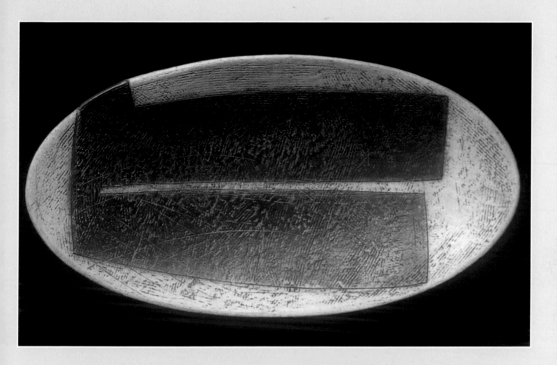

In my work I use various handbuilding processes, both alone and in combination. Which technique I use is a function of how it allows the form, or my idea of it, to evolve. Slabs afford a more immediate sense of the whole vessel, which I then modify with knife and paddle – a different way of finding form than the incremental bottom-to-top process of coil-building.

For platters and open bowls, slabs are the means by which I troll the space between two dimensions and three. What begins as a drawing on a shape becomes a form, with a horizon line and a skin that contains, however shallowly, a space. I love to watch and work with this transformation, which always develops in surprising ways.

This platter began as a textured drawing roughed out on a slab and laid over a bisque mould. Once it had stiffened into a three-dimensional form, the real work began: refining the edge and internal shapes in relation to

Untitled Platter *by Mary Barringer (USA).*
Stoneware, with slips and glaze,
6 x 53 x 28cm. © THE ARTIST

each other, selectively adding or removing texture, and paddling the contour inside and out. When the piece was leatherhard, I painted slip on: a dark or strong-coloured layer to set the 'cast' of the subsequent colours and graphically heighten the texture, and then a lighter one. These were followed, after the bisque firing, by up to six layers of coloured slip, in which I homed in on where the piece seemed to be leading me regarding colour, contrast versus a unified composition, and the visual weight of various parts of the piece. It is a time-consuming business, but I am making discoveries and decisions right up until the end, which keeps the process lively and infuses my 'surface work' with some of the energy that used to be confined to forming.

101

This kind of plate is made upside-down on a square piece of hardboard (of the size you want). The lump of clay you use should be wedged well and then beaten out with a wooden hammer and at the same time the outer surface [the back of the plate] is shaped and finished – using available tools – for instance, a rolling pin and scraper. The surface can be stiffened – dried out a little – using a gas flame or an electric blower. The plate is then turned over and hollowed out. It is not actually a slab

Plate *by Hans and Birgitte Börjeson (Denmark). Salt-glaze stoneware, 60 x 60cm.*

PHOTOGRAPH BY OLE AKHØJ. © THE ARTISTS

technique, but is an easy way of shaping a plate – as an alternative to using a slab over a plaster mould. The idea of beating the clay with a wooden hammer comes from the way of making saggars in the 'old days' – 'saggar making bottom knockers'.

A bone-dry clay cylinder with an impressed pattern is rolled over a wet slab making lines of raised dots. (A slightly irregular shape and a loose bolt shaft provide the desired looseness.) The length of the roller controls the width of the diagonals. The slab's curve is created by propping the edges with round wooden dowels. Four square feet are attached when the clay is leatherhard; thick white slip is brushed over the drying slab. When the slab is stiff, a metal scraper is used to reveal the dot pattern.

Diagonal Dot Plate *by Warren Frederick (USA). Stoneware, scraped white slip, milky-to-rusty glaze, 29 x 3cm. Reduction fired, 18-20 hours in an up-draught propane kiln; (almost) Orton cone 9.*

PHOTOGRAPH: WARREN FREDERICK. © THE ARTIST

Because the glaze is responsive, milky-white where thick and a rich brown-orange if thin, the slab is dipped and drained to create an irregular glaze thickness.

CONCLUSION

The process of creating flat slabs of clay is so very basic that they have been used in many different contexts throughout the history of ceramics. When the flat slabs are produced in multiples and formed into regular shapes, they can be used to spectacular effect, as can be seen in Islamic architecture for instance, where large areas of the surfaces of buildings, both exterior as well as interior, are often covered in clay tiles.

The creation of clay tiles or slabs on a large scale can be an event that involves and unites many people. In May 1993, artists and musicians from thirty-five countries world-wide assembled at Northern Arizona University (NAU), in Flagstaff, Arizona, USA, to participate in the 'World Clay Stomp', and create *The World Peace Mural* over a period of four days. Each artist brought fired pots from their home country with them to Arizona, which were ground into grog before being mixed with clay. Members of the audience at this event participated by helping to 'stomp' the clay with their feet, thus blending the clays of the world, while the musicians performed.

Once the clay was mixed, it was pressed into large wooden frames and the artists then created individual tiles, which were later fired in the two large woodfire kilns at the University. The completed mural, which measures 24m in length by 3m in height (80 x 10ft), was subsequently installed at the Prairie Peace Park in Lincoln, Nebraska, where it can be seen from the interstate highway.

The 'World Clay Stomp' at which the tiles for this mural were created, was a joint venture between members of NAU staff – Professors

ABOVE: *Individual tiles for* The World Peace Mural *unpacked from the 'Tozan' woodfire noborigama kiln at the ceramics facility, Northern Arizona University, Flagstaff, Arizona, USA, 1993.*

OPPOSITE: *Detail showing a section of* The World Peace Mural *installed at the Prairie Peace Park in Lincoln, Nebraska, USA.*

PHOTOGRAPH BY PETER SALTER

105

LEFT: **The World Peace Mural** *installed at the Prairie Peace Park in Lincoln, Nebraska, USA,* **24 x 3m.**

PHOTOGRAPH BY PETER SALTER

BELOW: *View of* **The Walking Wall Mural** *in front of the ceramics area at Northern Arizona University.*

PHOTOGRAPH BY JASON HESS

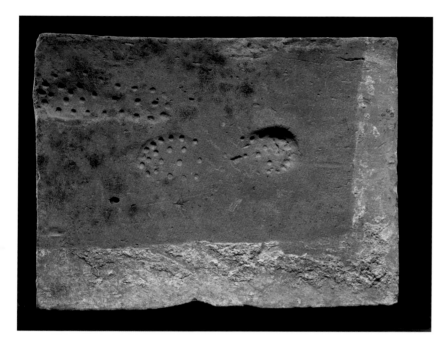

Romano-British flat slab with impressions of two boot prints. Length 41cm.

Don Bendel and Paula Rice and Director of the NAU Museum, Joel Eide, and 'Clay – A Healing Way', a non-profit organization based in Wisconsin, which is headed by Joel Pfeiffer, a long-time organizer of Clay Stomps.

Inspired by the 'World Clay Stomp', tiles for another, much smaller mural, were created during a ceramics conference at NAU in 1996. Individual tiles were made from clay on which those attending the conference walked, leaving impressions in the soft clay. This *Walking Wall* mural is located in the University grounds in front of the ceramics area.

These murals, architectural works made from slabs of clay, together with the diverse range of slab-built ceramics described and illustrated throughout this book, are indicative of the vast potential for personal expression that is possible using variations of this most fundamental of clay-forming techniques.

BIBLIOGRAPHY

Books

Barker, David, *Slipware*
(Shire Publications, Princes Risborough, 1993)

Brown, A.C. and Catlin, H.W., *Ancient Cyprus*
(Ashmolean Museum Publications, Oxford, 1986)

Cort, Louise Allison; Farhad, Massumeh; and Gunter, Ann C., *Asian Traditions in Clay – The Hague Gifts*
(Smithsonian Institution, Washington, DC, 2000)

De la Bédoyère, Guy, *Pottery in Roman Britain*
(Shire Archaeology, Princes Risborough, 2000)

Freestone, Ian, and Gaimster, David, *Pottery in the Making – World Ceramic Traditions*
(British Museum Press, London, 1997)

Gault, Rosette, *Paper Clay*
(A & C Black, London, 1998)

Karageorghis, Vassos; Vassilika, Elena; and Wilson, Penelope, *The Art of Ancient Cyprus in the Fitzwilliam Museum, Cambridge*
(The A.G. Leventis Foundation, 1999)

Karageorghis, Vassos, *The Cyprus Museum*
(C. Epiphaniou Publications, Nicosia, Cyprus, 1989)

Kerr, Rose, and Wood, Nigel, *Science and Civilisation in China*, Volume V:12
(Cambridge University Press, 2004)

Laidman, Roberta, *Slab Building Illustrated – A Technical Guide for the Ceramic Sculptor*
(Laidman Dog Press, 1995)
(The paperback edition of this book is now out of print, but it is available as a downloadable PDF file from which a paper copy can be made.
See: http://www.laidmanproductions.com)

Mansfield, Janet, *Ceramics in the Environment – an International Review*
(A & C Black, London, 2005)

McGarva, Andrew, *Country Pottery – Traditional Earthenware of Britain*
(A & C Black, London, 2000)

Medley, Margaret, *The Chinese Potter – A Practical History of Chinese Ceramics*
(Phaidon Press, 1989)

Ming, Bai, *La Porcelaine de Jingdezhen – Savoir-faire et techniques traditionnels*
(bi-lingual French-English edition)
(La Revue de la Céramique et du Verre, France, 2005)

Minogue, Coll, *Impressed and Incised Ceramics*
(A & C Black, London, 1996)

Minogue, Coll, and Sanderson, Robert, *Wood-fired Ceramics – Contemporary Practices*
(A & C Black, London, 2000)

Moorey, P.R.S., *Archaeology, Artefacts and the Bible*
(Ashmolean Museum Publications, Oxford, 1969)

Moorey, P.R.S., *The Ancient Near East* (Ashmolean Museum Publications, Oxford, 1987)

Morris, Desmond, *The Art of Ancient Cyprus* (Phaidon Press, 1985)

Robison, Jim, *Large-scale Ceramics* (A & C Black, London, 1997)

Sanders, Herbert H., with the collaboration of Kenkichi Tomimoto, *The World of Japanese Ceramics* (Kodansha International, 1971)

Simpson, Penny; Kitto, Lucy; and Sodeoka, Kanji, *The Japanese Pottery Handbook* (Kodansha International, 1979)

Vainker, S.J., *Chinese Pottery and Porcelain – from Prehistory to the Present* (British Museum Press, 1991)

Walker, C.B.F., *Cuneiform*, in *Reading the Past* series (British Museum Press, London, 1993)

Wilson, Richard L., *Inside Japanese Ceramics – A Primer of Materials, Techniques and Traditions* (Weatherhill, 1995)

Wondrausch, Mary, *Mary Wondrausch on Slipware* (A & C Black, London, 2001)

Wood, Nigel, *Chinese Glazes* (A & C Black, London, 1999)

Additional Titles

The Burrell Collection (Harper Collins Publishers in association with Glasgow Museums and Art Galleries, 1996)

Catalogues

Watson, William, *The Genius of China* (Catalogue of an exhibition held at the Royal Academy, London, UK, 1973)

Academic Journals

Vandiver, P.B., *Sequential Slab Construction – A Conservative Southwest Asiatic Ceramic Tradition c. 7000–3000 BC*, in *Paléorient*, Vol 13/2, 1987 (Published by Editions du Centre Nationale de la Recherche Scientifique, Paris)

CD Roms

Pierides Foundation Collection, Volume 1, Pierides Foundation Museum, Larnaca, Cyprus (Produced by The Cobb Institute of Archaeology, Mississippi State University, USA, and Concept House Inc.)

Magazines

Ceramics Art and Perception, Australia (Published quarterly) www.ceramicart.com.au

Ceramics Monthly, USA (Published monthly except July and September) www.ceramicsmonthly.org

Ceramic Review, UK (Published bi-monthly) www.ceramicreview.com

Ceramics Technical, Australia (Published twice a year) www.ceramicart.com.au

Clay Times, USA (Published bi-monthly) www.claytimes.com

BIBLIOGRAPHY

The Journal of Australian Ceramics,
Australia (Published three times a year)
www.australianceramics.com

*The Log Book – International Wood-fired
Ceramics Publication*, Republic of Ireland
(Published quarterly)
www.thelogbook.net

New Ceramics, Germany
(Published bi-monthly)
www.neue-keramik.de

Pottery Making Illustrated, USA
(Published bi-monthly)
www.potterymaking.org

La Revue de la Céramique et du Verre, France
(Published bi-monthly)
www.revue-ceramique-verre.com

The Studio Potter, USA
(Published twice a year)
www.studiopotter.org

GLOSSARY

Anagama – or tunnel kiln. A single chamber through-draught woodfire kiln.

Cryolite – a mineral used in frits and glazes.

Engobe – a liquid used to coat clay surfaces which, unlike a slip, can contain non-clay materials.

Grog – ground fired clay available in a variety of different grades or sizes used to give texture and strength to raw clay bodies.

Hallam fireclay – a type of fireclay available in Australia.

Kaolin – china clay. Kaolins are white-firing clays.

Lithium – used as a flux in glazes.

Molochite – the trade name for calcined china clay used as a refractory in clay bodies.

Nepheline syenite – a feldspathoid mineral used in high-temperature glazes.

Noborigama – a multi-chamber climbing woodfire kiln.

Shino – a high-temperature glaze – often pink or orange in colour – containing nepheline syenite.

Slip – liquid clay used in decorating (with oxides or other colouring pigments added).

Terra sigillata – a very fine slip. The term is used to describe pottery coated in such slip, the surface of which is burnished before being fired.

Tunnel kiln – a single chamber through-draught woodfire kiln, also known as anagama.

Wads – shapes made from a mixture of refractory materials (fireclay, alumina, sand, etc.) used to support ceramic work, particularly in saltglazing, sodaglazing and woodfiring, to prevent it from fusing to kiln shelves.

Index